Following Jesus
Overcome the World

Following Jesus
Overcome the World

CARLA BIGHAM

XULON PRESS

Xulon Press
2301 Lucien Way #415
Maitland, FL 32751
407.339.4217
www.xulonpress.com

Unless otherwise indicated, Scripture quotations taken from
the King James Version (KJV)–*public domain*.

Scripture quotations taken from the Holy Bible, New
International Version (NIV). Copyright © 1973, 1978, 1984,
2011 by Biblica, Inc.™. Used by permission. All rights
reserved.

Printed in the United States of America.

ISBN-13: 978-1-5456-6979-2

Contents

Chapter 1

A Lost World

Christians need to understand how to survive and how to overcome the world. We cannot fix what we don't recognize or acknowledge. Reading this book, I hope you get a clear understanding of why the world is distressed. I hope you find renewed hope and commitment to our Lord and Savior Jesus Christ. Throughout this book, I have carefully placed scriptures to support the statements that I have made. Some of these scriptures are familiar favorites, and others may be lesser known. They are critical to the writing and essential in the life of every Christian. Please take your time and read and reread these passages closely to reap their benefits. Often, I am trying to express something in each passage that drew me to it. I pray these passages guide you as you continue your walk of faith.

1 Peter 1:18–1:19

For you know that it was not with perishable things such as silver or gold that you were redeemed from the empty way of life handed down to you from your ancestors, but redeemed with the precious blood of Jesus Christ, a lamb without blemish or defect.

Reading the scriptures, it tells us that our ancestors handed down an empty way of life. An empty way of life is a life that has no real meaning or purpose. I hope to expose the emptiness that many people experience living self-centered lives in the present time. Most people are entirely unaware of how things have progressed to our current state.

Philippians 2:21

For everyone looks out for their own interests, not those of Jesus Christ.

Everyone looks out for their own interests and live selfish unproductive lives. It is this mentality that has created the present condition of humanity.

Philippians 2:14–2:16

Do everything without grumbling and arguing, so that you may become blameless and pure, "children of God without fault in a warped and crooked generation." Then you will shine among them like stars in the sky as you hold firmly to the word of life. And then I will be able to boast on the day of Christ that I did not run or labor in vain.

In reading the scriptures, they tell us that it is possible to become blameless and pure in a warped and crooked generation. It is possible to live as a child of God in a warped and crooked generation. The scripture also tells us to hold firmly to the word of life. "The word of life" refers to the scriptures in the Bible. Simon Peter once called them the words of eternal life.

The Diamond Within

This book is designed to help you understand that we must end selfish desires and pursue God's will instead of our own. The pain and suffering that we all experience purify us and help us work out any problems in our souls. Suffering helps us get over our egos and enables forgiveness. It helps us discover that true riches are not money or things, but eternity with God. Instead of seeking temporary things of this world we should be seeking God. The pain and pressure purify our souls and are necessary to develop godliness. Godly suffering guides us and turns us away from worldliness. For many years, I have compared it to a diamond formation. Scientists have different theories as to how diamonds form. They agree that it starts with carbon and occurs in the earth mantle at least 90 miles deep. They also say that it involves intense heat and great pressure. Diamonds also need to be brought to the surface with great force. I have often felt that God was using the pressure from this life to get the impurities out of me. If it were not for intense heat and pressure, a diamond would not form. I used to say that I felt like a lump of coal that God was turning into a diamond. I have discovered that it is carbon and not coal as many people believe. The example still holds; the process is necessary to allow change and bring about purification. Many people cannot understand why there is so much pain and suffer in the world today. There are two reasons for this:

1) **Humankind turned away from God.** We call to God for help but continue to follow the world. We turn to worldly knowledge instead of godly knowledge. We do not have the godly knowledge to handle all the pain and suffering that humans have inflicted upon themselves.

2) **Humankind has allowed Satan to trick and deceive him.** It is our worldly desires that Satan uses to entice us. It creates selfishness and greed within us.

There are diamonds and pure souls within all of us. We need to allow God to purify our souls. I believe that the pain and suffering are this intense because man's corruption has led us to this point. It is only through following Jesus and seeking God that we will be able to turn this around. Following Jesus is our only hope. It is better to become a diamond than to own one.

There may be no hope for our children and grandchildren if Christians do not mature and take a stand. This book is designed to awaken Christians to get them to understand the battle at hand. We are fighting for our children and future generations. Make no mistake about the damage being done because we have put brilliant minds in charge without teaching them morals or ethics. We have paved the way for greed and corruption. Christians have stepped aside or turned their heads too many times. Every time we go along with something immoral, we are allowing the world to be shaped by evil. You may argue that your livelihood depends on making exceptions that you know are morally wrong while on your job. Every time we make an immoral exception, we are shaping the future for many generations. I believe it is the ethical responsibility of all Christians to take a stand for God. Christians cannot agree with Satan. We have more control than we think and should strive for a plan that allows us to follow Jesus in a corrupt world. We cannot sell our souls or those of our families for the American dream. The truth is that it has become a nightmare. We have all been programmed to seek money and possessions. I believe the government initially thought it would be good to educate us and prepare us to help businesses prosper. They failed to teach morals or godly values in public schools. What you see today is a direct result of greed created by man.

You may feel that it is hard to live godly in a corrupt world. I will try to simplify this for you in future chapters. God would not ask us to do it if it were not possible. It is called being a Christian, and it means following Jesus even through suffering. I believe that our purpose for being on this planet is to mature and work out our salvation. We need to overcome the world, our egos, and selfishness. We need to learn to love one another genuinely. It is going to be a journey and will require work and sacrifice.

You may ask who I am and what right do I have to suggest such things? I am a Christian. I believe that Jesus Christ died for my sins and I have received him. All biblical quotes come from the New International Version of the Bible (NIV). I have no credentials. I am just a godly woman who believes that Christians need the truth because we are being deceived.

Since 1990, I have worked in manufacturing as both a manager and as an employee. I have witnessed in person the decline of the American way of doing business and the treatment of employees. There are massive amounts of greed and corruption consuming this country. Greed and destruction are what happens to a country when we take God out of schools and promote education without morals and ethics. Our children are in an education system void of ethics or morals. Satan has been pursuing our families while we have been pursuing the American dream.

Christians must prepare to protect our families. We need to understand how to put on the full armor of God and to stand against evil. We must recognize those wrong choices hurt all humankind. We all suffer because we all reap what we all sow. Begin by paying attention to situations in your life. Your soul is not dead just malnourished and inactive. Reading the word of God and having an active prayer life will breathe new life into our souls. You will notice things that you let slide, compromises that seem reasonable in the business world. We must prepare ourselves because we cannot walk into a battle unprepared. Expect resistance because Satan doesn't want what is godly for our children.

A Lost World

We as human beings do not realize what has been happening over time. We are born into a corrupt world. We deal with generations of pain and sin that our ancestors have passed on to us. We have been tricked and deceived for many generations. Satan doesn't fool us in an obvious way because he needs us to agree with him. Our agreement is why it is necessary for him to use deceit. He tricks us slowly and methodically over time. He doesn't offer us a fair deal that we can understand. Satan tells us that everyone in the world has a great job and that everyone is more important than we are. Satan tells us that being a mom or housewife isn't an important job. What Satan wants us to believe is that being an executive is more important than being a father. He wants us to look at the world and see the education, the new house, and the new cars. While we desire all these things, he has been systematically stealing our children.

Look at the drug problems with children today. Our children are in so much pain that they turn to drugs. They have been given things instead of time and values from their parents. Our children are unarmed and unprepared to deal with pain and temptation. Most parents believe that their job is to feed, clothe, and educate a child — you know, help them to be successful. Unfortunately for our children, we have not taught them to be godly, honest, or ethical. We failed to teach them to be happy or grateful. We have not prepared them to deal with pain or disappointment or to endure suffering. We did not teach them to care about anyone but themselves. We did not teach them about God, Jesus, or the Holy Spirit. We did not inform them that there is hope or teach them to love one another.

I believe that when Satan tricked the government into taking God out of our schools, it was a turning point of epic proportion. We can now see what effect turning our backs on God has created for our children. We have traded their futures for things that we wanted for ourselves. We made a deal with the devil. This book was designed to develop strong and mature Christians. Christians that will stand for God and fight fearlessly. It's not too late to open your eyes and your Bibles. It is time to become aware and to be courageous. We need to stop looking for a spiritual leader for our families and become a spiritual leader for our families.

Luke 12:15

Then he said to them, "Watch out! Be on your guard against all kinds of greed; life does not consist in an abundance of possessions."

We were all born into sin and worldliness. Our parents meant well but were deceived and could not predict the outcome of their choices. Generations have been lost trying to find a way to be successful in life. We are confused as to the definition of successful. The world defines success as having money, possessions or power. To meet the world's definition of success, we only need to possess things or power. We don't need to be decent, honest or have ethics. We could acquire these earthly possessions with malice or deceit. The world's plan is not God's plan or definition of successful. He wants more for us than to be successful by possessing things that will fade away. God wants us to have a moral compass and be godly people. God wants us to live by godly standards. We must clearly understand that worldly standards are not godly standards.

We are born into the world innocent and unprepared. We learn how the world functions and accept it as normal. What our parents and families do seem to be normal for most of us. Some parents are much more damaged and unable to provide even worldly standards for their children.

When we go to school, they train us to focus on the future. They ask us, "What do you want to be when you grow up?" or "What college would you like to attend?" School can be challenging because we are already in a system. We are rewarded for getting the best grades. We are defined as successful or unsuccessful using a pass-or-fail system. There is also a lot of social pressure to fit in with the popular people. We are not celebrated for being the amazing individuals that God created us to be. We are placed in this human-made environment in which states decide the curriculum. We were innocent children, and we followed the rules blindly. We trusted our parents, our teachers, and the law. We believed that they were there to protect and guide us. Their idea of being successful meant money and power. They wanted this instantly, and they learned to get it by any means. What we did not realize was that all these opportunities and possessions came with a huge price tag. We did not develop godly knowledge at the same pace as worldly knowledge. Many spiritual teachers were unprepared because they did not teach us that we needed to suffer and to mature. As the world seemed to get easier and faster, there was no need to suffer or mature. Since we had all the worldly possessions, we turned away from God. We were so engrossed in ourselves and possessions that we failed to realize that we needed God for everything. We lacked the depth and understanding of being a Christian. We lost the ability to love sincerely. We wanted everything for ourselves and wanted it instantly.

Our legal system and our government have also been shaped by manipulative minds that sought power and greed. Laws today have nothing to do with truth or justice. Corrupt attorneys and lawmakers protect the interest of the wealthy and corrupt. What will happen to humankind without godly morals?

Luke 11:46

Jesus replied, "And you experts of the law, woe to you, because you load the people down with burdens they can hardly carry, and you yourselves will not lift one finger to help them."

We became out of balance when we put worldly knowledge above everything else. We gave our minds worldly information but failed to seek godly information at the same time. It was like handing a loaded gun to someone without a conscience. The mind is self-serving and can seek power and money without concern for others. The mind's purpose is to gather information and process that information. Its function is self-preservation and to identify how things relate to us in the world. The results of strengthening the mind without godly knowledge are seen in every home, business and our government. It touches every life whether directly or indirectly. Greed and selfishness harm all of humanity, and we all pay the price. It even harms our world through pollution and damage to the environment.

Life without God is frightening, and it should scare all of us. I can't tell you that it's all going to work out. Everything went out of balance when we put the mind above our soul and body. It went out of balance when we put ourselves and possessions before God. Can you imagine if we had followed godly knowledge and principles? Imagine a world where we loved one another and genuinely cared for each other, and there was no selfishness or greed. That is how far off course we are as human beings.

Greed is also harming our physical bodies. When we look at the food industry, we can see that their concern is to make money. Worldly minds seeking profit have stripped our foods and created unnatural foods that make us ill. We have businesses manufacturing our food with no nutritional value for our bodies. When we look at the obesity in our country, we can see some of the health issues. We are all aware of cancer and diabetes, to name a few of the health problems. The pharmaceutical companies are making billions at our expense.

Our spiritual health is compromised by increasing worldly knowledge without godly knowledge. Christians are weak and ill-fed, and they have few defenses against the attacks of the devil. Christians need to understand that we are not doing enough. Our minds are still worldly, and our bodies are still worldly. Our souls are trying to survive in this human-made environment. Many Christians go to church on Sundays to search for guidance and offer praise. Churches were never meant to be your only connection to God. Our churches guide us but cannot replace a personal relationship with God. To develop godly character is going to require studying the Bible. The work that we do one on one with God is where real growth begins. Think of it as trying to earn a master's degree while only attending a two-hour lecture once a week. We have an opportunity to grow so much during the rest of the week. If we think for a moment that this is enough to protect our families from the world or Satan, we are sadly mistaken. We have no defenses without knowing the word of God.

We need to seek a personal relationship with God and must put God first. The reason we put God first is out of love and respect for him. The other reason is that our relationship with him defines who we are and how we handle ourselves in the world. We need to understand the scriptures to defend ourselves and teach our children values. It is time for Christians to do the work necessary for a full understanding of God's word. I am talking about gaining a good grasp of the Bible and understanding the messages in the scriptures. I am not suggesting that we save everyone around us. We cannot teach what we do not know. The relationship is a personal one between you and God. In this way, we are not offending others and turning them away from God. We are the pupils and have so much to learn. Our purpose is to learn the word of God and live as an example and then to instruct others gently. We must stop compromising who we are and hold ourselves to a godly standard instead of a worldly standard. The command to love one another was not optional. If we had followed that command, the world would be a different place today. We are fighting for the futures of our children and grandchildren. How important are our worldly possessions now? We have not only prized worldly possessions above God but also above our children and grandchildren.

Romans 15:4

For everything that was written in the past was written to teach us, so that through the endurance taught in the Scriptures and the encouragement they provide we might have hope.

This is your wake-up call! Change is not going to be easy and will require learning the word of God. Picture a person extremely lazy and out of shape training to go into battle. We have not understood that we were in a battle. To be a Christian means to follow Jesus Christ and his teachings. The only way to live a godly life is to put God first. We must accept Jesus Christ as our Lord and Savior and follow his example. The only way to understand God's will is to study his word and develop a personal relationship through prayer. We begin to understand the importance of putting God first as we begin the practice. We start to see worldly deceptions because of biblical principles. We will feel when something is wrong or questionable. It is a process that becomes easier when we are working with God. We may question whether we have time to make a difference. With our last breath, we should be working toward the glory of God.

Education balanced with morals and ethics can be a wonderful thing. When I speak of the problems with education, I am referring to education without godly ethics or morals. I know many people have worked hard for their degrees. I do not wish to offend anyone or take anything away from their hard work or school pride. Unfortunately, many people do not have ethics and morals to balance their educated minds. These are the people who I am speaking about whenever I speak of education. This concept may be hard to understand because people are closely identified with their degrees. It is how they define and view themselves. Only you know if you have ethics and morals are in balance with your education or degrees. We need to ask ourselves if we are seeking godly knowledge with the same commitment that we seek worldly knowledge. When we go to college, we are working toward a degree that should allow us to get a better job and more income. When we seek godly knowledge, it makes us better human beings. It creates a better world for our children and grandchildren. We must realize the true value of the lessons taught in the scriptures. We often think of God as a source we go to in times of trouble. Perhaps there would not be so many times of trouble if we considered him our first source of information.

Most of us believed that sending our children to school or college was a kind and loving thing. By worldly standards, it was a well-intended foundation for their futures. While focusing on the mind and education, we neglected to teach our children morals, ethics, and godliness. We helped our children do homework but failed to teach them godly values. We must be an example to our children, but we cannot teach them if we have not studied the word of God. If our children are self-absorbed and worldly, it is because we did not teach them to love others or to turn away from the world. We taught our children worldly values and left them morally empty. We should also instill good work ethics so they can learn this value while they are young. The only chance that we have for changing our future is to turn to God for help. This change requires a personal commitment in addition to studying the scriptures. We need to make prayer and reading the Bible a priority or remain defenseless.

After people graduate from college, they are often hired by worldly companies. They are required to meet manufacturing demands by any means. Most of these young people have not had the opportunity to develop people skills or understand the physical part of operations. Young graduates have not had an opportunity to work and often do not understand these requirements. Suddenly they are the boss, and they are commanding a large salary and will do anything to keep the position. Some of these young managers have not been brought up with morals or ethics, and they fall into an already corrupt company. Companies are eager to hire these young, naive people as managers because they can mold them into corruption. These young adults offer much less resistance than a mature person with ethics and morals.

1 Corinthians 15:33

Do not be misled: "Bad company corrupts good character."

Most employees are not treated very well and are not happy with their employment. Many people cannot leave because of financial commitments. It would do little good for them to find another job since this is the practice in most businesses. Today it is rare to find an ethical employer that treats employees fairly and honestly. There are people who get along wonderfully with this type of dishonest management. They are often promoted because they can play the game and have no problem with unethical practices. The future looks very bleak. We have created a system that is very corrupt and broken. Many corrupt managers oversee many situations that American employees face today. People today are promoted solely because of their education, and they lack the morals and ethics to lead. We are being led to fulfilling their agenda to get money and power. American workers are abused more today, and the laws are written by corrupt lawmakers to protect corrupt businesses. Our children and grandchildren will inherit the insane mess that we have created.

I call the ungodly managers running our country today "intellectual bullies." The reason I call them this is because they use their knowledge as a weapon. They feel superior to the average worker and form alliances with other corrupt managers. Often, the workers never have hope for ethical treatment. Most workers know that they are corrupt and offer little resistance for fear of losing their jobs. I have found that they have no defense against the truth. Courageous Christians baffle them because they cannot manipulate the truth. They are counting on our fear and passiveness to control our behavior. We need to educate ourselves on the scriptures to survive in this corrupt environment. If we do nothing against the abuse of power, our children and grandchildren will be their next victims. We cannot go to work with guns blazing and attack. The corruption is far and wide within these businesses. Often, companies and managers are very manipulative and have no intention of having policies of honesty and integrity. It is not fair, and it is not just. We cannot expect fairness or justice from morally bankrupt people. We need to learn defense through biblical scriptures as to how to carry ourselves at work. Christians need to be unafraid to make a stand when necessary and in a godly way. We cannot change our work environments overnight. These worldly dynamics have been forming over many years. We can choose to stay away from the rumors and inappropriate conversations. We can make ethical choices about who we are and where we stand. Pray for strength and guidance daily and especially whenever there is a difficult situation. It is difficult to be a Christian in a work environment that is worldly and sinful.

2 Peter 2:8–2:9

(for that righteous man, living among them day after day, was tormented in his righteous soul by the lawless deeds he saw and heard) if this is so, then the Lord knows how to rescue the godly from trials and to hold the unrighteous for punishment on the day of judgment.

Corruption is not just in manufacturing companies but throughout our country in many businesses and institutions. It has touched every part of our social structure and the business world. Corruption has found its way into our legal and our justice systems. Our laws are created by politicians that have been motivated by special interests or money.

God is alive and waiting for us to realize what we have created without him. We need to get on our knees and ask him to forgive us. We cannot get on our knees once and think that things will change. We need God to lead and guide us daily!

2 Timothy 3:1–3:5

But mark this: There will be terrible times in the last days. People will be lovers of themselves, lovers of money, boastful, proud, abusive, disobedient to their parents, ungrateful, unholy, without love, unforgiving, slanderous, without self-control, brutal, not lovers of the good, treacherous, rash, conceited, lovers of pleasure rather than lovers of God having a form of godliness but denying its power. Have nothing to do with such people.

In the scripture, it says having a form of godliness but denying its power. It says there will be terrible times in the last days. When we read the scripture describing how people will act in the last days, it sounds very familiar. Many people today are living this way. Many people have faith but are failing to do the work and understand what it means to be a Christian. Many people believe in Jesus Christ but have followed the world because of a lack of godly knowledge. People can have strong faith, but so much more is available and required.

Chapter 2
Maturing the Body of Christ

Ephesians 4:13–4:15

Until we all reach unity in the faith and in the knowledge of the Son of God and become *mature*, attaining to the whole measure of the fullness of Christ. Then we will no longer be infants, tossed back and forth by the waves, and blown here and there by every wind of teaching and by the cunning and craftiness of people in their deceitful scheming. Instead, speaking the truth in love, we will grow to become in every respect the *mature* body of him who is the head, that is, Christ.

Often when we read Bible scriptures, we don't recognize the true meaning or how it applies to our lives. The scriptures above describe the need for maturing. We have no unity because everyone cares only about themselves and their own desires. We have worldly knowledge but very little knowledge of the Son of God. To mature and attain the fullness of Christ, we need to have a deep and meaningful relationship with him. When we mature, we will no longer be infants tossed back and forth by the waves. When we mature, we can handle the waves and trials of life. We will not be blown here and there by every wind of teaching or by the cunning and craftiness of people in their deceitful scheming. When we are immature, we are easily manipulated by people who have selfish desires and schemes. The verse is not really about the waves and the wind. It refers to immature Christians that do not know the fullness of Christ. Christians need to mature to withstand the attacks and scheming of deceitful people. It is by learning godly principles by studying the Bible that we mature. It is only when we learn to speak the truth in love that we will grow in every respect to be the mature body of Christ.

James 1:22

Do not merely listen to the word, and so deceive yourselves. Do what it says.

Taking God for Granted

To take someone for granted means that we expect someone to always be available without thanks or recognition and to value them too lightly. Even worse than taking God for granted is using him in situations that benefit us and then turning from him when it is convenient to act worldly. With everything we do or say, we are either following Jesus

Christ or following the world. Our minds begin to justify situations to ease our guilt about choosing to be worldly. Christians are not maturing because they are not taking God seriously. God and heaven seem to be a distant far away idea. God is not an idea that has nothing to do with what is happening in your everyday life. God is alive and reigning and should have everything to do with our daily lives. We need to stop thinking of God as being in heaven separated from us by distance. If we believe that Jesus Christ died for our sins and have accepted him as our Lord and Savior, then the Holy Spirit lives within us now. We have been lost in the world and have not sought a personal relationship with God. We need to give God the attention and respect that he so rightfully deserves. We can develop a close and loving relationship with God through prayer and Bible study. We will adopt godly principles and be better able to serve and lead our families. Now that we understand how lost the world is, we must commit to seeking God. Many people can't understand why there are constant pain and suffering. We realize that we need God but not how much we need his love and guidance. Most people want him to ease the pain but not enough to give up their worldly desires. Basically, Christians want God to stop the pain and fail to understand that it is our own selfish desires causing the pain. To end the suffering, we must all turn away from the world and seek God with our whole hearts.

Our Choices

Magicians trick us by focusing our attention on one hand while the trick or deceit is actually happening in the other hand. We are being deceived because we have been focusing on loving things rather than loving God and one another. It is increasingly difficult to love one another in this day and age. We are very busy and in constant pain and under extreme pressure. There is very little relief or joy in the world. The question is, how do we stop the pain and the suffering? The first instruction is to love the Lord with our hearts, souls, and minds, and with all our strength. The other instruction is to love one another. Obviously, this means we all must change. The degree that humanity improves is dependent on how many people can turn away from their evil desires and turn to God. The greater the number of people who understand the importance of this change, the greater it will be.

Mark 12:30–12:31

Love the Lord your God with all your heart and with all your soul and with all your mind and with all your strength. The second is this: "Love your neighbor as yourself." There is no greater command than these.

Balanced Beginnings

Although some parents make their children the center of their universe, we are not the center of the universe. Being raised as the center of the family is well-intended love, but it creates a false reality. Believing that one person is more loved or important makes things distorted and out of balance. It fails to teach us to value and love others. It exaggerates our self-image and does not give us a clear picture of ourselves. We are damaged when we create a world that centers around us instead of around God. Our parents told us that we were special and could do anything. The truth is that we are nothing separate and apart from God. We are his children and need to understand his desire for us instead of seeking worldly desires. We were intended to seek God, our father, and not to think more highly of ourselves than we ought. We were designed to love one another and to care for each other's needs. It is possible to love your children in a healthy balanced way and to teach them respect and compassion for others. We will be doing them a service as they grow into compassionate people. Some children were not spoiled and may have envied the children whose parents did seem to have everything. It is far better to have humble possessions and to be balanced in our lives. Learning this as a child is very beneficial. Either way, it can be a struggle to try to find a clear path in the world today. Remember that the gate is narrow, which means that not many will find the way. Many may be unable to turn away from the world and toward God.

Laziness

Being spoiled and entitled as children has made life difficult for younger generations. When we add the worldly desire to have everything instantly, it compounds the problems. Most people do not want to wait for or work for anything. Children have not been taught to wait patiently or to work hard. They often aren't satisfied or don't feel a sense of accomplishment. The combination of Satan deceiving us and life coming at us so quickly has created a very stressful world. Our selfish desires combined with being lazy has increased the stress, and many feel overburdened. We need to make God a priority because it is his guidance that should control our actions in every situation. Our faithfulness to God determines our beliefs and develops our character. Our godly principles define how we treat our parents, spouse, and how we raise our children. The pain and suffering of this world are caused by humankind and self-inflicted. If we had put in the work to live godly lives, we would not all be suffering to this extent. Living in a world where people are putting money and power before God is extreme suffering for all human beings. We are putting things that will perish before God. We are also putting things before our families and before each other. We need to make a sincere effort to make God the number one priority in our lives. The Bible can be intimidating, but we can comprehend all of it when we continue to study the scriptures. It takes time to understand, and slowly all the pieces begin to fit when we continue to seek godly knowledge and principles. Please do not let fear or intimidation keep you from studying the Bible. Humanity cannot survive without godly knowledge. We pushed ourselves in school, and we can push ourselves to learn godly knowledge. We need to be determined and reorganize our time. We can stop accepting worldly commitments and prioritize our time. We can use our creativity and time management skills to glorify God.

Don't Want to Be Different

Many people have a fear of not fitting in or of being different. This fear comes from the world and not from God. The world teaches us that we should fit in and to worry about what others think. Keep in mind that it is mankind that created what we consider to be normal in the world. We need to distinguish what is from man and what is from God. A hint is that God is light and in him, there is no darkness. What a tragedy it is that we are trained to go along with and to fit into the world. The goal is to awaken Christians and help them to see that the worldly path cannot lead to God. Change can be difficult but is absolutely necessary because the worldly path leads to death and destruction. Read the next scripture very carefully.

It states that when we were slaves to sin, we were free from the control of doing what is righteous or moral. When we seek our own worldly desires, we do so because we do not hold ourselves to godly standards. The scripture also asks what benefit you reaped when you did the things that you are now ashamed of doing. When we do things in sin, there is never a benefit for humanity. When we do something against God, it hurts all of humanity. Sins are committed for selfish reasons and always harm others. When we live according to God's will, the benefits we receive are holiness and eternal life. The immediate benefit that we receive doing what is morally correct is that we no longer inflict pain on one another. We can see the value of living godly and loving one another in every area of our lives. We all reap what we sow.

Many people get caught up in the word *righteousness*. It sounds like something that we can never live up to because it seems perfect and unattainable. Knowing our own sins and worldly nature we feel that it is something unreachable for us. When we learn what the moral laws are, it gets easy to act accordingly. Being righteous is merely doing the right or honest thing. The only reason it seems confusing is that we do not have a clear understanding of God's word. Many people are caught living in the world claiming to love God, but they do not know him or his word. If we claim to love God, we must seek him diligently and learn his character and godly knowledge.

Worldly people do not know how to live a godly life because they just do not know. Many times, they have been abused or hurt by worldly people and have not been exposed to genuine godly people.They have not had true Christian examples or any training in godly behavior or scriptures. They simply do not know what they do not know. They only have worldly values and often turn to drugs or crime to manage the pain of living a life without God or hope. When Christians live godly lives and turn away from the world, they are genuinely lights for a lost world.

Romans 6:20–6:21

When you were slaves to sin, you were free from the control of righteousness. What benefit did you reap at that time from the things you are now ashamed of? Those things result in death!

Don't Want to Suffer

By living in the world, we have developed worldly minds. We expect things to happen instantly and easily. We do not want to wait or work for anything. Things happening so fast can actually harm us because it creates impatience and selfishness. The world delivers possessions very fast, and we do not develop the skills to mature. A few of the skills that we are missing are patience, kindness, and self-control. When any difficulty comes against us, we immediately suffer and fall apart. Usually, things are well again, and we do not suffer long. One would think that God is allowing all this ease and speed in life. I do not believe that it is God. It is man's mind creating these advances at warp speed. Many of these advances seem beneficial at first, but later we see the harm and destruction. There are many dangerous things that man is experimenting with at our expense. The world is coming at us so fast that we do not have time to develop the skills necessary to please God. Our computers, cell phones, and other devices speed our work and entertain us. They keep us busy and alone interacting with technology. How can we learn to love one another without a human connection? We are not developing any of the skills of communicating with each other. Our children cry and expect instant relief. Most children receive what they desire instantly. This does not create a loving or patient child. We need to understand that a Father that loves us must also teach and mature us. We need to grow and evolve beyond our selfish desires. We need a balanced value system and compassion. These values and compassion are often acquired through suffering. If there were no resistance in life, we would not be able to overcome difficulties and develop depth in our souls. The worldly person cannot perceive suffering as a blessing. When we view suffering from a selfish standpoint, we can only see our pain. When we view suffering from a godly point of view, we understand that we are overcoming obstacles and maturing. There is a vast difference between worldly suffering and godly suffering. Worldly suffering is pain that we inflict on each other because of greed and selfishness. Godly suffering is teaching us something to mature us to get worldly desires out of us. It is for our benefit and does not inflict pain on others. Think of disciplining one of your children. We love our children but often must tell them no when they want things that could harm them. It is a loving father that develops our character to be godly instead of worldly. Please understand that even Jesus suffered while he was in the world. Why do we think that we will not suffer or be persecuted? It is necessary to allow suffering to grow and mature and to develop the attitude of Jesus.

1 Peter 4:1–4:2

Therefore, since Christ suffered in his body, arm yourselves also with the same attitude, because whoever suffers in the body is done with sin. As a result, they do not live the rest of their earthly lives for evil human desires, but rather for the will of God.

Love of Money, Love of Things

We have been taught by the world that our success and identity are tied to our possessions. As a society, we believe that wealth and possessions somehow make us more important. Honestly, they do when we are worldly and have worldly standards. It is a worldly deception perpetuated by our greed. Identifying with possessions can keep us from identifying with God and with each other. When we value worldly possessions, we are identifying with worldly standards and ideas. The world is happy to bombard us with new things that will make us more important and make our lives easier. Loving things and money makes us selfish and worldly in nature. We fail to identify with God and are unable to love each other. We are consumed with acquiring more and more believing that it will make us happy. We can be happy and content living within our means. It is our worldly thoughts that make us feel like a failure if we have less than others. We are bombarded by commercials and signs that make us desire expensive possessions. Wealthy people are only successful by worldly standards. Wealthy people are not peaceful, fulfilled, or joyful as we are when we follow Jesus Christ. Worldly people are shallow and lack depth in their souls. A Christlike spirit is based on love and has depth and width. Worldliness is based in selfishness and greed and leaves you unsatisfied. If you are tired of shallow people and worldly possessions, it is time to seek a deeper relationship with God. Life has to be about more than possessions and selfish desires. Worldly desires and distractions keep us from finding a deeper meaning in our lives. Television and media distract and entertain but do not really enrich our lives. We need to be studying the word of God and commit to understanding the word of God. The new car and new house will both get old. Our bodies will age, and things of this world will pass. The work we do for God can change eternity for many people. It is time to decide how we will spend our time on this earth. Will we spend our time selfishly seeking worldly desires, or will we spend it wisely seeking God?

1 Timothy 6:9–6:10

Those who want to get rich fall into temptation and a trap and into many foolish and harmful desires that plunge people into ruin and destruction. For the love of money is a root of all kinds of evil. Some people, eager for money, have wandered from the faith and pierced themselves with many griefs.

Acceptance of the World

We often imitate the world believing that it is acceptable behavior. We have worldly examples all around us and very few godly examples. We have gone from not being allowed to see a married couple in the same bed to watching television with extreme sexual content and violence. I am concerned for our children today because they are accepting these standards as normal. The change happened over several generations so that we are desensitized to the increase of seduction and violence. Unfortunately, these are normal standards for the world and widely accepted. As Christians, we need to block these channels and enable internet protection for our children. We need to e-mail television stations and movie producers and tell them that we want some decent programming for our families. Look at the scandals in Hollywood, where pedophiles have been abusing children for decades. The actors say that they were groomed by people in power in the film industry. Is it any wonder that the same people in power have allowed so much violence and sex into movies and television? I am talking about children being subjected to ideas to which they would not naturally be exposed. We are allowing a greedy and perverted industry to have the power to decide what our families view. Their motivation is money, and they do not care about harming children. To keep making money, they have to increase the sex and violence to satisfy worldly people. How much farther will they go? We do not take the time to write to the people behind this because we accept this as normal. In the movie theaters, you can rarely find a movie that is not full of evil demons, violence, or sex. The world is lost and cannot self-correct. We as Christians must do something because worldly people do not see the problem. If we stop buying tickets and start blocking channels, we can make a difference. Again, if you are hoping for the world to self-correct, you are putting your hope in the wrong place.

Ephesians 4:17–4:19

So I tell you this, and insist upon it in the Lord, that you must no longer live as the Gentiles do, in the futility of their thinking. They are darkened in their understanding and separated from the life of God because of the ignorance that is in them due to the hardening of their hearts. Having lost all sensitivity, they have given themselves over to sensuality so as to indulge in every kind of impurity, and they are full of greed.

Lack Self Control

We lack self-control because our society is fast-paced and requires instant gratification. We are living in an increasingly lost world, and many people are suffering. Satan does not want us to develop the skills necessary to grow as Christians. Life has become difficult, and many have developed very short fuses. We often fail to see that other people have needs because of our own selfishness. Greed and selfishness have indeed hardened our hearts. We will never develop beyond worldliness if we continue to allow ourselves to be instantly gratified. We will never grow as a mature Christian until we turn away from the world and seek God with our whole hearts. We need to do the work and develop true godly spirits. We need to love God and one another instead of loving ourselves or possessions. The Holy Spirit will guide us as to what we lack in self-control. We must first acknowledge our weaknesses and then start doing the work to change. Begin by asking for forgiveness and add daily prayer. Begin researching scriptures to strengthen and mature as a Christian. We cannot merely accept the worldly behavior and continue living in sin. We need to stop allowing our minds to manipulate the truth. We cannot justify ungodly behavior as normal or make excuses any longer. Truth needs no excuses or allows any manipulation. This will require suffering through the pain instead of avoidance or self-medicating.

Need for Solid Food

Every Christian needs to work out their own salvation. We have allowed ourselves to be influenced by a corrupt world. We need to stop allowing ourselves to seek worldly desires and commit to godly lives. A church may be a great place to begin, but the journey is not over. We need so much more of God than a few hours on Sunday. We must pay attention to how we spend our time. Use your time and resources to understand scriptures. We will only grow equal to the amount of effort that we put forth. We can all see what happened to the world when we failed to lead godly lives. It is critical for humanity to seek and find godly morals and principles. Many Christians believe that they are doing enough by attending church once a week. Ministers are guides and not responsible for our salvation. Our salvation is a personal relationship and for us to work out with God. Churches have kept the word of God alive and form a valuable foundation. We as individuals must also seek a much deeper relationship with God our Father. What Jesus did for us is personal, and the Holy Spirit within us is personal. We are all on our own journey, and we must seek our own salvation. *To seek* means to go in search or try to find something. Seeking redemption is work, and we must define the target. It will be work to get the worldly thoughts and desires out of us and to replace them with godly thoughts and desires. In church and on your own diligently seek God and his son Jesus Christ. The Holy Spirit will guide you on your journey. Often the world is so loud and coming at us so fast that it is difficult to imagine another way of life. A godly way of life is possible but only when we turn away from the world and seek him with our whole hearts. Many of us seek a spiritual leader for our families, and it is well-intentioned. It is time to become a spiritual leader for our families. God needs mature Christian parents and grandparents to be living examples to children.

James 1:27

Religion that God our Father accepts as pure and faultless is this: to look after orphans and widows in their distress and to keep oneself from being polluted by the world.

We are to keep ourselves from being polluted by the world. We as Christians need to be responsible for developing our own relationship with God. We need to understand what it means to follow Jesus Christ. We are not getting the spiritual food that we need to mature. We should be developing the maturity to stand against the world. How can we put on the full armor of God if we do not understand what it is? We need Christians to get beyond themselves and beyond worldliness. We need mature Christians to stand for God. When we study the Bible, we will understand the godly principles necessary to overcome the world. It is impossible to seek God when we are seeking the world. When we allow ourselves to let go of the world and devote ourselves to God, it gets much more attainable. Trying to do both is ultimately impossible. It is a personal decision that each one of us must make for ourselves. We cannot have it both ways. We cannot act worldly while calling ourselves Christians.

Hebrews 5:13–5:14

Anyone who lives on milk, being still an infant, is not acquainted with the teaching about righteousness. But solid food is for the mature, who by constant use have trained themselves to distinguish good from evil.

Our solid food is found in the scriptures. When we were immature Christians, we were given milk because it was easy for us to digest. Solid food requires feeding ourselves. The solid foods that we need as Christians are to seek godly knowledge from the scriptures. With the constant use of godly knowledge, we can distinguish good from evil. There are many other tools that we must learn to use, such as love, goodness, and self-control.

Chapter 3

Live as Foreigners

1 Peter 2:11

Dear friends, I urge you, as foreigners and exiles, to abstain from sinful desires, which wage war against your soul.

1 Peter 1:17

Since you call on a Father who judges each person's work impartially, live out your time as foreigners here in reverent fear.

Living as a Foreigner

Try to imagine what a foreigner feels like in a different country. They are away from their homeland and everything that is familiar. Foreigners adapt to living in new places because it is necessary to survive. We must not forget that we are Christians that live in the world, but it does not mean that we must live in a worldly way. The scriptures warn us to live out our time as foreigners in reverent fear. Living with reverent fear means to stand in awe and to respect the power of God. We are to have respect for God and live a life that demonstrates his love to others. We have been warned to abstain from sinful desires that wage war against our souls. The scriptures are written to give us guidance and to warn us of the dangers in the world. We live in the world but still choose how we live according to our beliefs.

Most people can understand the difference between right and wrong. It seems that some people are naturally caring while others are not compassionate. I am sure that our environments influence our development. If we were mistreated as children, those experiences shape our views and character. If we were loved as children, it also influences our opinions and personality. Even if our childhood was relatively functional, we could still have experienced significant pain as teenagers and adults. We have to be determined to live as Christians regardless of what the world chooses because we are a light for a lost world.

John 12:46

I have come into the world as a light, so that no one who believes in me should stay in darkness.

Just because everyone else acts, a certain way does not mean that it is acceptable for a Christian. Being a

Christian, we already have a sense that things are not right in the world. We cannot deny the many things that we see daily. The truth is that we are all suffering. We focus on our own pain and fail to recognize that pain and suffering are worldwide. We have a sense of being separate from the world, and at the same time, we must function as part of the world. We know that something is very wrong but continue because we don't know how to fix the problems. It is like not being able to see the forest for the trees. We are in the middle of the pain and chaos. No one wants to admit that they are in pain and do not have a perfect life. When we pretend to have happy lives, it keeps us from effectively dealing with the problems. Everyone presents a happy facade because we are afraid to expose our unhappy lives. The truth is that we are all inflicting great pain on one another. We are unable to have compassion for others' suffering because our hearts have become calloused. This keeps us divided and unable to comprehend how truly massive the pain has become. It is our own pride and ego that perpetuates our mass suffering. Living a Christian life in a corrupt world is possible. Many of our family members, friends, or work associates may be worldly. We may feel that it is normal to live as they are living. This normal behavior is not the behavior that God is seeking in his children. We need to make a firm decision as to whether we follow the world or God. We cannot do both.

We must be willing to work diligently with God. It is a process that requires Bible study and faithfulness. We need to fix our inside damage before we can save anyone or change the world. We have developed worldliness one compromise at a time. We must stop compromising our beliefs and be committed to being a Christian. Think of the oxygen mask falling in front of you on an airplane. They tell you to put your mask on first so that you can help other people. We are not prepared to lead others because we have all been lost in the pain and suffering. Understanding the problems in the world and the determination to stand as a Christian can make all the difference. We have failed to see the danger of following the world. When we open our eyes and see the deception, we can choose a different path. We no longer have to live our lives unaware and helplessly suffering. We can follow Jesus with determination and choose to live godly instead of worldly.

2 Timothy 2:25–2:26

Opponents must be gently instructed, in the hope that God will grant them repentance leading them to a knowledge of the truth, and that they will come to their senses and escape from the trap of the devil, who has taken them captive to do his will.

It is a frightening thought that when we sin, we are actually doing the will of the devil. The scripture says that we will come to our senses and escape the trap of the devil when we repent. I know it can seem frightening, but we can live according to our true beliefs. We do not have to save the world or try to be the workplace monitor. At work, we can be quiet and observe the world. Many of the people in our work environments do not follow God. We can pray for them and can be a living example of a Christian. Pushing our beliefs usually turns non-believers away, and they are unable to receive any message. We should not be a person who calls ourselves Christians and then behave as non-believers. As we mature, we will be able to help non-believers. We cannot guide them properly until we have matured. The scriptures remind us to gently instruct opponents. It is interesting that the scripture refers to worldly people as opponents. Living in a world full of people who do not share your beliefs can be very confusing. Some of our opponents can be our loved ones. This does not mean that we live in a war zone where we are trying to convert people. It is all about our individual journey and beliefs. Our loved ones do not have to share our beliefs, and we can still love those people. We can love them without agreeing with their worldly decisions and lifestyles. We do not have the right to force our opinions. God has given us free will and a right to choose for ourselves. Just as we have the right to believe in Jesus Christ, they have the right to decide for themselves. Our real power lies in living a truly Christian life and being a living example of godliness. We can love them without judging them because we are not their judge. Christians should be a light in a very lost world. The decision to accept Jesus Christ as their Lord and Savior is a personal choice, and it is their decision. We are each responsible for our own growth and maturity.

Ephesians 4:22–4:24

You were taught, with regard to your former way of life, to put off your old self, which is being corrupted by its deceitful desires; to be made new in the attitude of your minds; and to put on the new self, created to be like God in true righteousness and holiness.

It takes time to mature and is often difficult to let go of our old selves. It may be painful to deny ourselves worldly things that we desire. It can be very difficult to deny a habit that we have allowed in the past. If we do not take authority over these desires, they will have power over us. There are two kinds of suffering. Worldly suffering is the kind that we inflict on one another for selfish reasons such as greed or evil desires.

An example would be if someone was unfaithful and caused you to feel great pain. The other kind of suffering that we experience is to teach and mature us. An example of godly suffering would be to turn away from a worldly desire and suffer through the temptation. This can be difficult, but after we overcome the desire, we can take authority over it. When we deny ourselves worldly desires, it feels painful. The good news is that after we suffer through it, we can get authority over these desires. I don't want to make this sound easy because it is not. It does not mean that we will not be tempted in the future. The more authority we have over something, the less it can control our behavior. We can tell ourselves no the instant a temptation comes into our mind. The sooner we deny the temptation, the stronger our resolve will be in denying the temptation. Our minds will attempt to weaken our resolve. We must dismiss the temptation as soon as we say no and not allow our minds to negotiate. It may help to say no out loud in a firm voice (when you are alone) when temptation begins. Forcefully tell yourself no inside when you are not alone. Two things happen when we say no out loud. First we are standing firm against temptation, and second, we are speaking in a commanding voice. It is very powerful, and we give our spirit a voice louder than the thoughts of temptation. It is as if we bring the temptation into a place where it cannot hide. It is amazing to see the power that we have when we bring things to light. When we stop negotiating and firmly refuse to entertain the temptation, we have real power. When we maintain our faith, we will be able to resist when tempted. Overcoming temptation will take commitment. If we fail, we must strengthen our resolve to find ways to change our patterns. We cannot think about the thing we desire and let it control our lives. We cannot allow our minds to struggle and create more pain and desire. When we feel overwhelmed by temptations and desires, we must focus on the strength that God gives us to overcome. When we continue to focus our attention on the temptation, we give it power. Often, instead of feeding into the desire, we can find an enjoyable distraction to break the cycle. Redirecting ourselves in prayer or calling a friend are options. Our thoughts and desires are very powerful. By breaking the cycle of temptation and habit, we can discover a new way of life. We must not follow our minds when they get locked into destructive desires. Often, our minds have such a tight grip on us that we don't realize that we are being tempted. Often, we do not realize that there are many more choices available. Don't underestimate the power of our spirit boldly saying no and being firm in our decision.

1 Corinthians 10:13

No temptation has overtaken you except what is common to mankind. And God is faithful; he will not let you be tempted beyond what you can bear. But when you are tempted, he will also provide a way out so that you can endure it.

Our worldly desires have power over us because we do not have the skills to overcome their temptation. We know that certain desires have strongholds in our lives. We have given in to the temptation so many times that our response is almost automatic. We have little resistance because we do not understand that we have the power to resist. This cycle is almost automatic because we have had no resistance in the past. The word *resistance* means refusal to accept or comply with something. When we say no to temptation, we need to make it a firm refusal. We cannot allow any room for misinterpretation. We must not allow or comply with the temptation under any circumstances. No means no, and we cannot allow any room for negotiations. We are often like children that have never been told no and have not considered self-control as an option. We tend to repeat the same scenarios and patterns in our lives. We need to change things up and look for new interests and friends to break the cycle. When we love God and accept Jesus Christ, we will be filled with the Holy Spirit and will be guided past our temptations. God will work the worldliness out of us, and we will then have a godly nature. The Holy Spirit will guide us according to God's will and not our own. We begin to discern what is coming from our ego or the world and what is from God. Our motives for doing anything will be a crucial indicator and will always be a reliable guide. Always ask yourself why you are doing something and whom it benefits. Do you want to do something to get famous or have money? These are worldly and selfish motives. When we love God and want to serve him regardless of the outcome, we have a pure motive and a pure heart. Our Father and our Lord see our hearts and our motives.

Proverbs 16:2

All a man's ways seem innocent to him, but motives are weighed by the Lord.

Your salvation is a personal matter to work out between you and God. The more we grow and mature the more we will be able to assist our families. We will also be an example to friends and coworkers. How can we help someone to develop into a mature Christian if we do not know the way ourselves? We are all given a choice to believe and to love God. We are given a choice to believe that Jesus Christ is our Savior and died for our sins. We are free to believe in the gift of the Holy Spirit. It is a personal journey, and we need to decide what we believe. No one can do this for us, and we cannot do it for anyone else. As parents, we want our children to spend eternity in heaven, but it is ultimately their choice. Instead of setting worldly examples we can guide them by setting Christian examples. It is our responsibility to mature and seek God. God is waiting for us to wake up and realize the incredible plan that is waiting for us. This is eternity that we are talking about; it is so worth the work.

Putting on the Full Armor of God

To prepare for the hardships and battles, we need to understand how to protect ourselves. This may require some social adjustments. When the Bible tells us to love one another, it means in a balanced way. We cannot go to work loving everyone because we have a very complex society. There are many types of personalities and potential problems. The love that God is talking about is respecting and helping people through difficult times. Encouraging one another through faith and compassion. We are not to gossip or cause others to fall in any way. We need to be a loyal and honest friend and nothing more. We do not have to be friends with the people who tell dirty jokes or spread rumors. We don't have to go to the bar for a drink to be social. We can be social without participating in the worldly drama. This is especially true if you are married or have children. If you are married, be careful not to allow work associates into your personal life. Being too friendly may cause problems or ruin your marriage. Focus your time on sowing into your family instead of meeting coworkers after work. If you want a loving, supportive family, then be a loving, supportive mother or father. We will reap what we sow into our families. Anything leading us away from our family is an evil desire. We need to take the time to fix our family problems instead of turning to the world when things get difficult.

Ephesians 6:13–6:17

Therefore put on the full armor of God, so that when the day of evil comes, you may be able to stand your ground, and after you have done everything, to stand.

Stand firm then, with the belt of truth buckled around your waist, with the breastplate of righteousness in place, and with your feet fitted with readiness that comes from the gospel of peace. In addition to all this, take up the shield of faith, with which you can extinguish all flaming arrows of the evil one. Take the helmet of salvation and the sword of the Spirit, which is the word of God.

As Christians, we lack preparedness and godly knowledge. Many Christians have no idea how to prepare themselves or their family for the trials in the world. The scripture above gives us a general description to prepare us for battle. If we had been reading the scriptures, we would understand the instructions precisely. The belt of truth buckled around our waist shows us to stand firm in the truth. The breastplate of righteousness protects us because we always do what is right and honest. When we know the scriptures, we will have peace and our feet will always be ready. Our shield of faith is our faith in Jesus Christ. The helmet of salvation proves that we are saved by our belief in Jesus Christ our Lord and Savior. Our sword of the Spirit is the word of God. We can only learn and understand these things by studying the scriptures. This information and protection exist nowhere but in the scriptures. We must live and work in an unstable environment, and godly knowledge helps us to survive. When we read the scriptures, we can clearly see the difference between godly and worldly. We rely on our own interpretation in situations instead of seeking the answers in the Bible. Every problem that exists today has already been addressed somewhere in the Bible. With all of our advances in technology, the problems are coming faster. It may benefit you to find a website that has the Bible and allows searching of particular words or phrases. If we have a problem such as judging others, we can enter that phrase and read scriptures on that subject. Use the tools and seek godly knowledge diligently. We stumble and fall because we do not see the pitfalls. The only way to see the pitfalls is to study, and they will be revealed to us. We begin to build a base of knowledge and of wisdom. It does not happen overnight, but with consistent use, it will develop.

Begin by telling the truth every time. The mind will jump in and want to come up with a lie to manipulate a situation. Let your godly spirit rule and do not allow the mind to manipulate the truth. If we do something wrong, we need to accept responsibility. Telling the truth also keeps us in check because when we cannot lie out of situations. We will be less likely to do wrong or corrupt things when we are accountable. A person who lies never accepts responsibility and often blames others. Start doing what is honest even if the rest of the world is dishonest. Trust that God uses difficult situations to teach and mature his children. It takes commitment and awareness to understand when we are following the world and when we are following Jesus. This is why reading the Bible is so important, we cannot live godly lives unless we understand God's will and word.

Keep Your Thoughts on God

It is difficult to live in the world when your heart belongs to God. We know that the things that we are seeing are corrupt and wrong. We see people all around us who are in a great deal of pain and suffering. We need to understand that man's sin created this corruption by agreeing with the devil. We need to stop being distracted in this world and focus on God. This decision not only affects your life but affects all of our lives. When we choose to do something wrong, we selfishly inflict pain on someone else. We all need to do what is godly every time, without exception. We were deceived and may not have understood what was happening in the world. Each of us has a choice to make because we now know what is happening in the world. Now we know how things got so far out of balance. Do we contribute to the corruption, or do we turn to God? The main way the devil tricks us is by getting us to compromise and accept worldly standards. We need to keep praying and studying and live according to God's will. Living according to our own will is not the answer. Tell me how many godly people do you know? How many worldly, damaged, and selfish people do you know? Our worldly way is broken and not working. Imagine a world with godly people. Life would be joyful and not this constant state of suffering.

Colossians 3:1–3:2

Since, then, you have been raised with Christ, set your hearts on things above, where Christ is, seated at the right hand of God. Set your minds on things above, not on earthly things.

Accept suffering as God working out our worldliness. Every time we suffer, we learn more about our true motives and our real character. It can be painful, but growth is impossible without suffering. We would never mature past the point of a spoiled child without suffering. Think of suffering as growing pains. In our society, we self-medicate at the first sign of suffering. We may self-medicate with alcohol, legal drugs, or illegal drugs. There are many other forms of running away. On the other side of our pain is growth, maturity, and godly character. We need to remember that fear does not come from God. Damaged and wounded people have inflicted pain in all of our lives. But we can forgive them, and we can accept the pain. If we do not face the pain, we are stuck in that point and cannot move forward. If we accept the pain, it loses its power, and we are free to move forward. We can push through the pain, and we will develop as strong Christians.

1 Peter 4:12–4:13

Dear friends, do not be surprised at the fiery ordeal that has come on you to test you, as though something strange were happening to you. But rejoice inasmuch as you participate in the suffering of Christ, so that you may be overjoyed when his glory is revealed.

Many of us are surprised and confused by the fiery ordeal that has come on us. These things come on us to test us and help us to mature. Often, we feel like saying "Why me?" because we see others seemingly doing well. The truth is that many others are suffering and in pain. We feel like it is only us because we focus on ourselves and other people pretend that their lives are perfect. Often, what we see is really a mask that people put on to protect their pride. You may have a friend or relative who suddenly left their spouse. It seems odd to you because you believed that they had the perfect family with no problems. These life-shattering events usually are not sudden. Your friend may have lived with the problems for years but kept them hidden. People are so self-absorbed and care so much about what others think that they live false lives. Pretending something is perfect does not make it perfect. Hiding the truth from friends and family does not make it any less real. Being honest and not fearing other people judging us can be freeing. It can be exhausting to keep putting on a happy face for the world. Your real friends will love and support you through hardships. No one has a perfect life, and we have all been damaged in this world.

Hebrews 2:17–2:18

For this reason he had to be made like them, fully human in every way, in order that he might become a merciful and faithful high priest in service to God, and he might make atonement for the sins of the people. Because he himself suffered when he was tempted, he is able to help those who are being tempted.

Jesus understands our struggles and temptation because he became fully human so that he could be a loving and understanding Lord. Jesus suffered and was tempted so that he could help us through our struggles and temptations. That he would lower himself to be human and suffer everything for us gives us a glimpse of his love and grace. His death on the cross was the atonement for our sins so that we could be forgiven. It is not too late to be grateful for his sacrifices and to follow his teachings.

Chapter 4

God with Us

We have allowed the scale between right and wrong to be tipped in the wrong direction for many years. Although past generations have been unable or unwilling to take a stand, it is time. Christians can no longer go along with what is going on in the world. One principle will always hold true: we reap what we sow. We failed to sow godly values, and we are reaping pain and misery throughout the world.

Galatians 6:7–6:8

Do not be deceived: God cannot be mocked. A man reaps what he sows. Whoever sows to please their flesh, from the flesh will reap destruction; whoever sows to please the spirit will reap eternal life.

Since humanity has sown to please the flesh, we are all reaping destruction. It makes no sense because sowing from the spirit allows us to reap eternal life. We have failed to connect the dots and to understand the consequences of our choices. The harvest of what we have been sowing may be more than human-kind can manage. It feels as if the stresses of life are squeezing us into a very tight corner. Joy seems very rare in these troubled times. We have been at the mercy of worldly choices and corruption because we have allowed it. We failed to stand for what was right. We failed to arm ourselves with godly knowledge, and we failed to seek God. The Bible tells us that the word of God is alive and active. When we get beyond our-selves, we must realize that the Bible was written to guide and instruct people. Why is it that people fail to see the value and wisdom available in the scriptures? Obviously, they were trying to warn us not to follow a path of destruction. The world is living as if there are no laws or right or wrong. Allowing the world to be filled with greed and power has made it a very hostile environment. It is not only hostile for Christians but all humankind. We must understand that the world is not the world that God planned but a legacy of sin passed onto us by our ancestors. We are born innocent but born into a very sinful world. We as Christians are trying to overcome the world and mature at the same time. It may sound like it is too much to bear, but it is not impossible. When we mature, stay away from sin, and focus on making godly choices, it gets much more achievable.

Romans 1:28

Furthermore, just as they did not think it worthwhile to retain the knowledge of God, so God gave them over to a depraved mind, so that they do what ought not to be done.

The scripture warns us that we did not think it worthwhile to retain the knowledge of God. We are all paying the price for that decision. The scripture above mentions people being given over to a depraved mind. *Depraved* means to be morally corrupt or wicked. Many people are living their life with a depraved mind doing things they shouldn't be doing. We only need to turn on our television or phone to see the next story of how someone harmed another person. It seems our leaders and government have no clue as to why things are so bad. They do not understand why things are so bad because they have worldly minds and have no godly knowledge. So many people have made choices to follow the world. It appears that it has been this way for generations. This did not happen overnight or by accident. We have been selfish and self-serving. We believed that the natural course of life was to go to school, get married, buy a house, have children, send them to school, accumulate wealth, and seek entertainment. It often did not happen in that order, but that was the American dream. Notice that you do not see the words "seek God" or "serve God" in the dream. Notice that you do not see "suffer" or "serve anyone but ourselves and our family." Unfortunately, some people do not even serve their families; they only serve themselves.

Acts 17:27

God did this so that they would seek him and perhaps reach out for him and find him, though he is not far from any one of us.

Knowledge Based on Scriptures

I am focusing on the teaching of the New Testament. I need to go back to the Old Testament occasionally to find the right scripture. The hope is to help Christians mature and seek a deeper relationship with God. The goal is to help them overcome obstacles that are keeping them from growing. I use many scriptures in this book. I use scriptures to support my statements and to teach the scriptures to people unaware of their existence. It is critical that any Christian teaching is supported by scriptures and be based on the belief in Jesus Christ. The world has been damaged by people not following the word of God. Christianity is based on the belief in Jesus Christ and follows his teachings.

Matthew 22:29

Jesus replied, "You are in error because you do not know the Scriptures or the power of God."

Many people are confused about God the Father, Jesus Christ, and the Holy Spirit. I can only point to the scriptures to describe each of them. Again, these are a few selected scriptures, and there are many more to study. It is imperative to study the scriptures because when we learn bits and pieces, we can be confused. Christians need to have a deep understanding of biblical teaching. We need this information to live our lives. Eternity is, of course, a significant factor in following Jesus. Many have failed to make the connection that if we do not mature and develop a godly character on earth, many will not have an eternity in heaven. The teachings of Jesus show us how to live on earth and prepares us for eternity.

God Created the Earth

Genesis 1:1–1:2

In the beginning God created the heavens and the earth. Now the earth was formless and empty, darkness was over the surface of the deep, and the Spirit of God was hovering over the waters.

A Virgin Gives Birth to Jesus Christ Our Lord and Savior

Matthew 1:21

She will give birth to a son, and you are to give him the name Jesus, because he will save his people from their sins.

Matthew 1:23

"The virgin will conceive and give birth to a son, and they will call him Immanuel," which means "God with us."

Jesus Called His Twelve Apostles

Matthew 10:2–10:4

These are the names of the twelve apostles: first, Simon (who is called Peter) and his brother Andrew; James son of Zebedee, and his brother John; Phillip and Bartholomew; Thomas and Matthew the tax collector; James son of Alphaeus, and Thaddeus; Simon the Zealot and Judas Iscariot, who betrayed him.

The Crucifixion of Jesus Christ

John 19:18

There they crucified him, and with him two others — one on each side and Jesus in the middle.

Acts 5:30

The God of our ancestors raised Jesus from the dead — whom you killed by hanging him on a cross.

Jesus Died for Our Sins

1 Corinthians 15:3–15:5

For what I received I passed on to you as of first importance: that Christ died for our sins according to Scriptures, that he was buried, that he was raised on the third day according to Scriptures, and that he appeared to Cephas, and then to the twelve.

The Gift of the Holy Spirit

Acts 2:38–2:40

Peter replied, "Repent and be baptized, every one of you, in the name of Jesus Christ for the forgiveness of your sins. And you will receive the gift of the Holy Spirit. The promise is for you and your children and for all who are far off — for all whom the Lord our God will call." With many other words he warned them; "Save yourselves from this corrupt generation."

It may seem confusing, but with faith and the knowledge of God's word, it becomes clear. We need to get close to God by understanding his word and believing in his son Jesus Christ. I have been baptized and believe that we all must be baptized. We are then filled with the Holy Spirit and begin living a godly life. We will feel guided by his spirit when hardships come. There will always be trials and difficulties even for Christians. The difference is that we will have the knowledge to endure trials and mature through hardships. These trials increase our faith and understanding. When we begin to live for God, we begin to see the sadness and shallowness of worldly people. We will have depth in our souls and understand that worldly living is meaningless. Serving God has true meaning because we love God and Jesus Christ and are filled with the Holy Spirit. We then walk in faith, peace, and love. We care about other people and are no longer selfish. We speak the truth and have no desire to deceive anyone. We will still come under attack, but we have the godly knowledge to survive. We will always be tempted and live among worldly people. The more we seek God, the stronger our knowledge and armor to resist the devil and the world will be. I hope you are beginning to see that loving and serving God is not just a religious act. It has real value for every part of our lives. It has real value and shapes the world and determines how we treat one another. It is a labor of love and a joy to have a personal relationship with God. Worldly people cannot comprehend this relationship because they believe it is too stifling. They think it will make them feel constrained or oppressed. People assume they would be constrained or oppressed because they do not want to give up their worldly ways. They cannot comprehend the joy, love, and freedom that comes from following Jesus. We are separate and apart from the world, and we must live that way. God comforts and guides us as we grow and mature. Worldly people cannot understand the peace and joy that mature Christians develop.

James 3:16–3:17

For where you have envy and selfish ambition, there you find disorder and every evil practice. But the wisdom that comes from heaven is first of all pure; then peace-loving, considerate, submissive, full of mercy and good fruit, impartial and sincere.

As Christians, our suffering has a purpose; it matures and develops us. We develop a godly character and learn to submit to God's will. We are rewarded on earth for developing godly character and for living godly lives. We live deeper more meaningful lives in every area. We are better parents, grandparents, and workers, and we live more stable lives. We don't need to drink excessively or use drugs to numb the pain of this world. With God, we can bear the pain and suffering. We are also rewarded in heaven. Unfortunately, worldly people suffer for nothing. All their selfish and greedy desires create so much suffering, and they do not improve as human beings. They may have money and a beautiful house, but if they have desired these things without loving God and accepting Jesus, they have suffered for things and have no eternal reward in heaven. It becomes bearable and honorable when we understand who we are suffering for and why we are suffering. We realize that God loves us and is trying to purify something in our character. After a while, we mature and are able to handle suffering and the attacks of the devil with godly character and wisdom.

It is truly freeing because we learn to overcome the world. Godly pain and suffering mature and develop us. Worldly pain and suffering do not develop our character or help us overcome the world.

When you read the next section, please understand that I am defining worldly people as people who do not know God or put his interests above the world. I define Christians as people who have accepted Jesus Christ and put God's interests first and are living godly lives. I am not judging anyone. I am trying to explain the difference between worldly and godly living. The personal relationship is between each person and God. I am only attempting to describe situations that keep Christians from seeking God. Human desires and life situations often hold our attention and keep us distracted. It is up to each individual to examine their personal relationship with God.

Matthew 16:26–16:27

What good will it be for someone to gain the whole world, yet forfeit their soul? Or what can anyone give in exchange for their soul? For the Son of Man is going to come in his Father's glory with angels, and then he will reward each person according to what they have done.

As Christians, we need to educate ourselves by reading the Bible and maturing with the lessons that we are being taught. We may feel that life is unfair.

Many people have more than others, and these people may be worldly. We wonder why, if God loves us, he allows us to suffer and let worldly people prosper. We are looking at it with a worldly view. They are prospering in worldly possessions, which will fade away. We believe that their lives are better because they have money, fame, or power. I am not saying that all rich, famous, or powerful people are worldly. They can have all these things and still put God first. I am speaking specifically of worldly people who do not put God first. I believe wealthy, famous, and powerful Christians have to work out their salvation with God differently than people who do not have money, fame, or power. The point is that whether you have wealth, fame, power, or none of them, you must always put God first. Live godly in all areas of your life. Money will not solve all of your problems. Fame and power will not solve all of your problems. It is my guess that being wealthy or famous may cause many problems that must be overcome. We all suffer in this world; God uses different circumstances to work the worldliness out of each of us. The real treasures that Christians are seeking are not of this world. The people who are tricked into only seeking worldly things will never spend eternity in heaven. We may feel that they are not suffering and enjoy a life of privilege. If they fail to seek God, they will spend an eternity suffering for that choice. Although God uses suffering to mature us, he loves us, and earthly ease and possessions are not our rewards. Worldly people also prosper because they steal from or manipulate the law against other people. They have no godly conscience that keeps them from doing these things. They seek worldly possessions and see nothing wrong with getting them, no matter whom they harm. As Christians, we cannot do that to people. We have the Holy Spirit to guide us to be able to discern right from wrong. We know what is of the world and what is godly. We do not steal or take anything that does not belong to us. We do not want ill-gotten gains and do not want to hurt people. Christians think very differently than worldly people. It may appear that they are favored now, but there will be a day of judgment. We would all have plenty if everyone was honest and made godly choices. There would be no greed or corruption in the world. We would help our brother instead of abusing him. The laws would be about truth and justice. Our society would not be in the terrible mess that it is in today.

Matthew 6:19–6:21

Do not store up for yourselves treasures on earth, where moths and vermin destroy, and where thieves break in and steal. But store up for yourselves treasures in heaven, where moths and vermin do not destroy, and where thieves do not break in and steal. For where your treasure is, there your heart will be also.

The things of this world are not our treasures. All earthly possessions will get old and be forgotten.

Treasures are things that we value. We must ask ourselves what we truly value and what we are allowing our hearts to seek. I cannot imagine how difficult it would be in this world without my faith and godly knowledge. Reading the Bible and the scriptures are so important and necessary. We should keep studying the Bible and make understanding it a priority in our lives. Create time by limiting worldly interests and make learning a way of life. Remember to keep things in balance because any kind of imbalance can lead to problems. When seeking a relationship with God and seeking godly knowledge, include it in your life in a balanced way. Many people can go to extremes with anything allowing it to create misery in their lives. When we understand godly scriptures and principles, we allow them in as part of our lives. For instance, telling the truth becomes a way of life. Loving one another becomes a kindness that we show to everyone. I am not suggesting that you lock yourself in a room and study the Bible and hide from the world. We can set a certain amount of time for studying the word of God and then begin to practice it in our everyday lives. It is not about knowing more or being godlier than others. Remember to love one another and instruct one another gently. Being a Christian is a lifestyle following the teachings of Jesus Christ. Just as he humbled himself to wash the disciples' feet, we should be humble when loving one another. It is not a competition as it is with the world. Our relationship with God and our commitment to following Jesus Christ are a journey, not a race. We should seek godly knowledge on a regular basis and mature as we diligently follow Jesus.

Chapter 5

Jesus Our Example

1 Peter 2:19–2:22

For it is commendable if someone bears up under the pain of the unjust suffering because they are conscious of God. But how is it to your credit if you receive a beating for doing wrong and endure it? But if you suffer for doing good and endure it, this is commendable before God. To this you were called, because Christ suffered for you, leaving you an example, that you should follow in his steps. "He committed no sin, and no deceit was found in his mouth."

In reading the scriptures, it clearly tells us that Jesus left an example for us to follow. It also tells us that we should follow in his footsteps. To suffer for doing good and to endure the suffering is commendable before God. The scriptures also tell us that we were called to this. We must remember that Jesus Christ suffered for our sins. Jesus walked this earth and committed no sin, and no deceit was found in his mouth. The idea of understanding the life and power of Jesus Christ is incomprehensible. I do not claim to have full knowledge of this. I can only quote what the Bible says about his life and teachings. I can use my own experience that faith and scriptures have taught me. I ask you to consider the importance of his conception, birth, life, death, and resurrection. There are a lot of scriptures in this chapter. I am using scriptures to highlight events of Jesus Christ. There are many more scriptures in the Bible regarding the life of Jesus Christ. I am trying to help struggling Christians to see the magnitude of Jesus and his impact on the world. No one can comprehend his majesty or power, I cannot even try. I am writing this to encourage Christians to take a good look at this timeless gift that still touches our lives to this day. Be diligent and read through these scriptures, put your heart and soul into understanding the importance of the words and their meanings.

What the term *Christian* means to me is to believe and accept Jesus Christ as your Lord and Savior and to be Christ-like by following his teaching and example. It means to believe in the birth, life and death, and resurrection of Jesus Christ. We need an understanding of what the Bible says about Jesus.

Our very calendar is based on his birth. Time before the birth of Jesus Christ was referred to as BC, meaning Before Christ. Time changed after the birth of Jesus Christ; it literally reset with his birth. The new era began with 1 AD. *AD* refers to *Anno Domini*, which is a

Latin term meaning "in the year of the Lord." Can you imagine a birth over 2000 years ago still having power today? I can think of no one else having any power like this in the world except for Jesus. All over the world, we base our calendars and understanding of time based on the birth of Jesus. This is a tiny example of his power and influence on the world to this day.

In the scriptures, there are descriptions of his conception, birth, life, death, and resurrection according to the apostle Matthew. I will highlight these events from the book of Matthew. I use many scriptures in this chapter. It is hard to get a clear view of Jesus because the scriptures are separated. I wanted to highlight the scriptures to get a clearer picture. Many people have an idea of who Jesus is or what he did for us. I hope that when we are reading these selected scriptures, we understand more clearly. Instead of thinking of Jesus in bits and pieces, I wanted to highlight his journey from conception to resurrection. There are many additional vital teachings of Jesus, and all of these should be read and appreciated. How can you express who Jesus was and what he did for us in one chapter? No measure could encompass the importance of Jesus Christ. I am only trying to inform readers who have not read them and to remind those that have read them of their significance.

Conception

Joseph Accepts Jesus as His Son

Matthew 1:18–1:25

This is how the birth of Jesus the Messiah came about: His mother Mary was pledged to be married to Joseph, but before they came together, she was found to be pregnant through the Holy Spirit. Because Joseph her husband was faithful to the law, and yet did not want to expose her to public disgrace, he had a mind to divorce her quietly. But after he considered this, an angel of the Lord appeared to him in a dream and said, "Joseph son of David, do not be afraid to take Mary home as your wife, because what is conceived in her is from the Holy Spirit. She will give birth to a son, and you are to give him the name Jesus, because he will save the people from their sins." All this took place to fulfill what the Lord had said through the prophet: "The virgin will conceive and give birth to a son, and they will call him Immanuel" (which means "God with us"). When Joseph woke up, he did what the angel of the Lord had commanded him and took Mary home as his wife. But he did not consummate their marriage until she gave birth to a son. And he gave him the name Jesus.

Birth

The Magi Visit the Messiah

Matthew 2:1–2:2

After Jesus was born in Bethlehem in Judea, during the time of King Herod, Magi from the east came to Jerusalem and asked, "Where is the one who has been born king of the Jews? We saw his star when it rose and have come to worship him."

Life

Escape to Egypt

Matthew 2:13–2:15

When they had gone, an angel of the Lord appeared to Joseph in a dream. "Get up," he said, "take the child and his mother and escape to Egypt. Stay there until I tell you, for Herod is going to search for the child to kill him." So he got up, took the child and his mother during the night and left for Egypt where he stayed until the death of Herod. And so was fulfilled what the Lord had said through the prophet: "Out of Egypt I called my son."

Return to Nazareth

Matthew 2:22–2:23

But when he heard that Archelaus was reigning in Judea in place of his father Herod, he was afraid to go there. Having been warned in a dream, he withdrew to the district of Galilee, and he went and lived in a town called Nazareth, so fulfilled what was said through the prophets, that he would be called a Nazarene.

John the Baptist Prepares the Way

Matthew 3:11

I baptize you with water for repentance. But after me comes the one who is more powerful than I, whose sandals I am not worthy to carry. He will baptize you with the Holy Spirit and fire.

Baptism of Jesus

Matthew 3:16–3:17

As soon as Jesus was baptized, he went up out of the water. At that moment heaven was opened, and he saw the Spirit of God descending like a dove and alighting on him. And a voice from heaven said, "This is my Son, whom I love; with him I am well pleased."

Jesus Is Tested in the Wilderness

Matthew 4:10–4:11

Jesus said to him, "Away from me, Satan!" For it is written: "Worship the Lord your God, and serve him only." Then the devil left him, and angels came and attended him.

Jesus Begins to Preach

Matthew 4:17

From that time on Jesus began to preach, "Repent, for the kingdom of heaven has come near."

Jesus Calls His First Disciples

Matthew 4:18–4:19

As Jesus was walking beside the Sea of Galilee, he saw two brothers, Simon called Peter and his brother Andrew. They were casting a net into the lake, for they were fishermen. "Come follow me," Jesus said, "and I will send you out to fish for people."

Jesus Heals the Sick

Matthew 4:23

Jesus went throughout Galilee, teaching in their synagogues, proclaiming the good news of the kingdom, and healing every disease and sickness among the people.

Jesus Heals a Man with Leprosy

Matthew 8:3

Jesus reached out his hand and touched the man. "I am willing," he said. "Be clean!" Immediately he was cleansed of his leprosy.

The Calling of Matthew

Matthew 9:9

As Jesus went on from there, he saw a man named Matthew sitting at the tax collector's booth. "Follow me." he told him, and Matthew got up and followed him.

Jesus Sends Out the Twelve

Matthew 10:1

Jesus called his twelve disciples to him and gave them authority to drive out the impure spirits and to heal every disease and sickness.

God's Chosen Servant

Matthew 12:18

Here is my servant whom I have chosen, the one I love, in whom I delight; I will put my Spirit on him, and he will proclaim justice to the nations.

Jesus Teaches in Parables

Matthew 13:35

So was fulfilled what was spoken of the prophet: I will open my mouth in parables, I will utter things hidden since the creation of the world.

Jesus Feeds the Five Thousand

Matthew 14:21

The number of those who ate was about five thousand men, besides women and children.

Jesus Walks on the Water

Matthew 14:25

Jesus went out to them, walking on the lake.

Jesus Feeds the Four Thousand

Matthew 15:38

The number of those who ate was four thousand men, besides women and children.

Peter Declares That Jesus is the Messiah

Matthew 16:16

Simon Peter answered, "You are the Messiah, Son of the living God."

Jesus Predicts His Death

Matthew 16:21

From that time on Jesus began to explain to his disciples that he must go to Jerusalem and suffer many things at the hands of the elders, the chief priests and the teachers of the law, and that he must be killed on the third day be raised to life.

The Transfiguration

Matthew 17:1-17:2

After six days Jesus took with him Peter, James and John the brother of James, and lead them up a high mountain by themselves. There he was transfigured before them. His face shone like the sun, and his clothes became as white as light.

Jesus Predicts His Death a Second Time

Matthew 17:22-17:23

When they came together in Galilee, he said to them, "The Son of man is going to be delivered into the hands of men. They will kill him, and on the third day he will be raised to life." And his disciples were filled with grief.

Jesus Predicts His Death a Third Time

Matthew 20:18–20:19

We are going up to Jerusalem, and the Son of Man will be delivered over to the chief priests and the teachers of the law. They will condemn him to death and will hand him over to the Gentiles to be mocked and flogged and crucified. On the third day, he will be raised to life!

Jesus Comes to Jerusalem as King

Matthew 21:7–21:11

They brought the donkey and the colt and placed their cloaks on them for Jesus to sit on. A very large crowd spread their cloaks on the road. The crowds that went ahead of him and those that followed shouted, "Hosanna to the Son of David!" "Blessed is he who comes in the name of the Lord!" "Hosanna in the highest heaven!" When Jesus entered Jerusalem, the whole city stirred and asked, "Who is this?" The crowds answered, "This is Jesus, the prophet from Nazareth in Galilee."

The Greatest Commandment

Matthew 22:37–22:40

Jesus replied: "Love the Lord your God with all your heart and with all your soul and with all your mind. This is the first and greatest commandment. And the second is like it: Love your neighbor as yourself. All the Law and the Prophets hang on these two commandments."

The Plot Against Jesus

Matthew 26:3–26:4

Then the chief priests and the elders of the people assembled in the palace of the high priest, whose name was Caiaphas, and they schemed to arrest Jesus secretly and kill him.

Jesus Anointed at Bethany

Matthew 26:12–26:13

When she poured this perfume on my body, she did it to prepare me for burial. Truly I tell you, wherever the gospel is preached throughout the world, what she has done will also be told, in memory of her.

Judas Agrees to Betray Jesus

Matthew 26:14–26:16

Then one of Twelve—the one called Judas Iscariot—went to the chief priests and asked, "What are you willing to give me if I deliver him over to you?" So they counted out for him thirty pieces of silver. From then on Judas watched for an opportunity to hand him over.

The Last Supper

Matthew 26:26–26:28

While they were eating, Jesus took bread, and when he had given thanks, he broke it and gave it to his disciples, saying, "Take and eat; this is my body." Then he took a cup, and when he had given thanks, he gave it to them, saying, "Drink from it, all of you. This is my blood of the covenant, which is poured out for many for the forgiveness of sins."

Jesus Predicts Peter's Denial

Matthew 26:34

"Truly I tell you," Jesus answered, "this very night, before the rooster crows, you will disown me three times."

Gethsemane

Matthew 26:37–26:39

He took Peter and the two sons of Zebedee along with him, and he began to be sorrowful and troubled. Then he said to them, "My soul is overwhelmed with sorrow to the point of death. Stay here and keep watch over me." Going a little farther, he fell with his face to the ground and prayed, "My Father, if it is possible, may this cup be taken from me. Yet not as I will, but as you will."

Jesus Arrested

Matthew 26:48–26:50

Now the betrayer had arranged a signal with them: "The one I kiss is the man; arrest him." Going at once to Jesus, Judas said, "Greetings Rabbi!" and kissed him. Jesus replied, "Do what you came for, friend." Then the men stepped forward, seized Jesus and arrested him.

Judas Hangs Himself

Matthew 27:4–27:5

"I have sinned," he said, "for I have betrayed innocent blood." "What is that to us?" they replied. "That's your responsibility." So Judas threw the money into the temple and left. Then he went and hanged himself.

Jesus before Pilate

Matthew 27:20–27:22

But the chief priest and the elders persuaded the crowd to ask for Barabbas and to have Jesus executed. "Which one of the two do you want me to release to you?" asked the governor. "Barabbas," they answered. "What shall we do then, with Jesus who is called the Messiah?" Pilate asked. They answered, "Crucify him!"

The Crucifixion of Jesus

Matthew 27:35–27:38

When they had crucified him, they divided up his clothes by casting lots. And sitting down, they kept watch over him there. Above his head they placed the written charge against him: THIS IS JESUS, THE KING OF THE JEWS. Two rebels were crucified with him, one on his right and one on his left.

Death

The Death of Jesus

Matthew 27:50–27:52

And when Jesus had cried out again in a loud voice, he gave up his spirit. At that moment the curtain of the temple was torn in two from top to bottom. The earth shook, the rocks split and the tombs broke open. The bodies of many holy people who had died raised to life.

Burial of Jesus

Matthew 27:58–27:60

Going to Pilate, he asked for Jesus' body, and Pilate ordered that it be given to him. Joseph took the body, wrapped it in a clean linen cloth, and placed it in his own new tomb that he had cut out of the rock. He rolled a big stone in front of the entrance to the tomb and went away.

The Guard at the Tomb

Matthew 27:65–27:66

"Take a guard," Pilate answered. "Go, make the tomb as secure as you know how." So they went and made the tomb secure by putting a seal on the stone and posting the guard.

Resurrection

Jesus Has Risen

Matthew 28:1–28:10

After the Sabbath, at dawn on the first day of the week, Mary Magdalene and the other Mary went to look at the tomb. There was a violent earthquake, for an angel of the Lord came down from heaven and, going to the tomb, rolled back the stone and sat on it. His appearance was like lightning, and his clothes were white as snow. The guards were so afraid of him that they shook and became like dead men. The angel said to the women, "Do not be afraid, for I know you are looking for Jesus, who was crucified. He is not here; he has risen, just as he said. Come and see the place where he lay. Then go quickly and tell his disciples: 'He has risen from the dead and is going ahead of you into Galilee. There you will see him.' Now I have told you." So the women hurried away from the tomb, afraid yet filled with joy, and ran to tell the disciples. Suddenly Jesus met them. "Greetings," he said. They came to him, clasped his feet and worshiped him. Then Jesus said to them, "Do not be afraid. Go and tell my brothers to go to Galilee; there they will see me."

The Great Commission

Matthew 28:16–28:20

Then the eleven disciples went to Galilee, to the mountain where Jesus had told them to go. When they saw him, they worshiped him; but some doubted. Then Jesus came to them and said, "All authority in heaven and on earth has been given to me. Therefore go and make disciples of all the nations, baptizing them in the name of the Father and the Son and of the Holy Spirit, and teaching them to obey everything I have commanded you. And surely I am with you always, to the very end of the age."

There are other events and other books in the Bible that give similar and other accounts of Jesus Christ. Again, I would encourage you to read the Bible to get a complete understanding.

Jesus set so many examples for us to follow. To become like Jesus Christ, we must understand his teachings. Jesus was setting an example in everything he did. To be Christians and to follow Jesus Christ may seem impossible because he was unblemished and we are so damaged by the world. Humankind has created destruction for ourselves and for the world. We may wonder how we can make a difference? When we begin to choose to do what is godly in our lives, we shine a light in the darkness and give the world hope. It starts with you. It feels like the darkness in the world is far and wide. We cannot focus on the darkness, we must become the light. Diligently choose to do what is right and stop following the world. Make a commitment to following the examples of Jesus Christ.

Matthew 19:26

Jesus looked at them and said, "With man this is impossible, but with God all things are possible."

Through our own strength and understanding, it is not possible to overcome the world. The good news is that with God, it is possible to overcome the world. When we follow Jesus, we have strength and faith to do what is necessary to turn away from the world. When we read the scriptures, we can search for the examples that Jesus set for us to follow. Our path is often unclear when we live worldly lives. Living worldly can cause our path to be very selfish and full of greed. Understanding that we should follow Jesus can define our path and clear all the confusion. Jesus must have believed that being baptized was very important. At the moment that he came up out of the water, it says that heaven was opened and the spirit of God descending like a dove alighting on him. It also says that a voice from heaven spoke. I am wondering if we understand the importance of baptism. Again, I would encourage you to follow the example that Jesus was setting.

John 3:5–3:7

Jesus answered, "Very truly I tell you, no one can enter the kingdom of God unless they are born of water and the Spirit. Flesh gives birth to flesh, but the Spirit gives birth to spirit. You should not be surprised at my saying, 'You must be born again.'"

Since we are born into a sinful world, we must first believe that Jesus died for our sins and accept him as our Lord and Savior. We then follow the example of being baptized in water and are filled with the

Holy Spirit. Jesus also gives us examples of how to overcome temptation. Jesus was tempted in the wilderness. Jesus was fasting for forty days and nights. Three times, the devil tempted him, and all three times, Jesus replied with answers about the word of God, not testing God, and worshiping and serving God. I wonder if we consider God in our decision when we are tempted. This one example could change everything.

Jesus suffered so much at the hand of man. He had the power to stop them at any point. He chose to endure the suffering to complete what he came here to do. Had he stopped at any point, we would not have an opportunity to be forgiven for our sins. I encourage you to accept trials and suffering; it is through them that we mature, develop godly character, and learn to love one another.

There is one final example that I wish to leave you with in this chapter because it also leads to the next chapter.

John 13:12–13:14

When he had finished washing their feet, he put on his clothes and returned to his place. "Do you understand what I have done for you?" he asked them. "You call me 'Teacher' and 'Lord,' and rightly so, for that is what I am. Now that I, your Lord and Teacher, have washed your feet, you also should wash one another's feet."

This example of the Lord washing the disciples' feet is a very strong example to us all. We need to humble ourselves and serve each other. Considering who Jesus was, it was a very humble act for Jesus to wash the disciples' feet. It also had to be very humbling for the disciples to have their feet washed by Jesus. Often, it is our pride that we must surrender to allow others to be able to serve. Many of us are good at serving people but find it difficult to allow someone to serve us. Others are good at allowing others to serve them but very bad at serving others. We truly need to find a balance that allows us to care for one another. We need to know that we are worthy of love and attention and value ourselves properly. We must also value others, care for them, and be cared for in return. Selfishness and greed keep us from loving one another selflessly, the way that we were intended to love. Balance in life is critical, and it takes very little to get out of balance. We are not to keep score, and one is not required when we genuinely love one another. When we meet each other's needs, nothing is lacking because we feel loved and valued. Worldly values and greed aren't important when our needs are being met, and we feel safe and secure.

When we speak of following the example of Jesus Christ, it means to be like Jesus Christ. When we think of following in his footsteps, it may be intimidating. We are talking about the Lord Jesus Christ, and the bar is set so high. This is why he came leaving us his example. Jesus tells us that he is our teacher and our Lord. We must learn from his teachings and value his sacrifices. To fully understand his teachings and sacrifices, it is imperative to study the word of God. There are no shortcuts, and we must work earnestly to seek God through the teachings of Jesus Christ.

Hebrews 11:6

And without faith it is impossible to please God, because anyone who comes to him must believe that he exists and that he rewards those who earnestly seek him.

John 7:16

Jesus answered, "My teaching is not my own. It comes from the one who sent me."

Many things are overwhelming for us to understand and overcome, but not impossible. People feel very overwhelmed in the world because they are handling life without godly knowledge. People are trying to manage their lives from a selfish worldly mindset. Can you imagine a life in which we had the godly knowledge to overcome evil? Can you imagine a world where we are not alone, and we could come to God for love and support? Can you imagine a world where we could love and support one another? The only way to get there from here is to follow the examples that Jesus provided and to pursue godly knowledge. The point is that we must earnestly seek God by following the examples set for us by Jesus Christ. The scripture tells us to seek him earnestly, which means with sincere and intense conviction. The question remains: Are we seeking God in earnest? Are we following the example of Jesus Christ? Are we seeking God seriously and putting in the effort to understand the lessons Jesus taught?

Chapter 6
Love One Another

John 13:34–13:35

"A new command I give you: Love one another. As I have loved you, so you must love one another. By this everyone will know that you are my disciples, if you love one another."

This is such a pure and simple command. Unfortunately, the world we live in today is not designed to encourage love. We need to understand the things of the world that keep us from loving one another. We also need to understand the things within us that keep us from loving one another. We are confused as to what love truly is, and how to truly love.

We are often left feeling exhausted and unable to comprehend why things are so miserable and why we are suffering. Our society teaches us to be selfish instead of training us to be decent and loving human beings. This has had a significant impact on how the world has developed. It has left us empty and shallow, seeking possessions and entertainment. It gets worse because most of our entertainment is very worldly and has to be increasingly violent or perverted to keep our attention. We follow our worldly thoughts that have been placed there through the internet, television, and other people. Our society's development is why we are all so miserable. We need to write to television stations, actors, and music artists to request more positive entertainment. We need mainstream entertainment that focuses and teaches the goodness in people. We can be entertained without watching murder shows depicting actual murders. The world has gotten so much more relaxed with sex scenes, and children are exposed to these images earlier and earlier. We need to realize that life is not just about entertainment. So many hours are wasted on entertainment. It is a distraction from the real work that we need to do in our lives. Entertainment has its place, but in excess, it gets out of balance and takes over your life. It seems like our society has gone from one extreme to the other with entertainment. They make movies that are incredibly violent, sexual, or demonic, or at the other extreme, very religious. Don't get me wrong; I enjoy the Christian movies that are produced. I applaud the godly producers and actors making these films. The only problem is that worldly people usually don't go see them. It is beneficial and uplifting for the Christian community. It would be great if people were also producing great films that had a chance to really get some ideas to worldly people. A story that just teaches us to love one another, or a movie about the importance of telling the truth. There has to be a way to reach wounded and hurting people who would not usually see a "Christian" film. There has to be a way to reach non-believers. Everyone staying far left or far right means that we cannot help one another. I am not suggesting that we compromise and meet the world or lower Christian standards. I am suggesting that we gently help non-believers. We were instructed to instruct them gently. We need to consider who they are and all the difficulties they have experienced. Their hearts may be hardened, but we must find a way to help lost people.

For many, life is filled with so much pain and suffering that they turn to drugs or alcohol to numb the pain. The television commercials will tell you that you cannot beat addiction. They want you to believe that you are weak and they will be happy to take your insurance payments. The fact is that people with addictions are genuinely suffering and hurting. At some point in their lives, someone deeply hurt or failed them. Someone may have failed to protect them from someone dangerous. Someone failed to teach them the skills to survive in this damaged world. As children, they may have been bought things while parents were too busy to spend time with them to teach them morals. Their parent may have had a drug problem and abandoned them as a child. The following are Christian suggestions and advice. I am in no way a substance abuse counselor. I feel that we need to look at the root causes of the pain to understand the problem. For now, I just want all those people hurting to know that I am sorry that we failed you so miserably. Just because the world was tricked and deceived does not mean that you cannot develop the skills you need to turn this around. Drugs and alcohol are not the answer, and they never were. My Christian advice would be for you to pray and ask others to pray for you. Forgive the people who hurt you and failed you and plan to rebuild yourself. I can promise you it will be difficult. The way the world is now, it will seem impossible. Find some support and do the work. Often when things are bad at home, we turn to people who are less desirable. Do not settle for this; you are God's child. You have been misguided and have not realized who you are or that God loves you. Do not let other people's failings define you. You can be whole even in this world. It will take work and commitment. It will take going through pain, suffering, and forgiveness. I don't know where we got the idea that we deserve an easy, fun-filled life — wait ... it was from television! Life is not easy; it is hard work. I am not a drug counselor; I am acknowledging that people are in real pain and need to do real work to manage their lives. Mankind created this environment for all of us. This was our own doing. It is possible to turn away from the world and to a loving God. We need to love God more than we fear the world. People lie and manipulate, and they have no problem hurting or taking advantage of other people. It is best to avoid these people and not allow them access to your life. Be careful who you invite into your life. Surround yourself with loving, honest, and supportive people. Don't stop looking until you find the support you need. When you have people who care, appreciate and value their sacrifices. Your character will affect your support because if you lie and manipulate, decent people will avoid involvement with you. Remember that you will reap what you sow. You have the responsibility to turn away from lies and manipulation.

We need to pray and ask that our sins be forgiven. We also need to ask God to remove all the sins committed against us that we have been carrying. Ask God to help you to forgive the people who sinned against you and caused you so much pain. We cannot allow the sins and the pain to define who we are in this world. While we pick up our cross and follow Jesus, we can put down the pain. Let the healing begin and choose love, peace, and joy. Releasing the person who caused our pain also frees us from the pain. It is painful, but we need to accept crucifying our ego and allow the suffering. We can let the part of us that is holding on to the pain to suffer through the pain. We cannot hide from the pain with drugs, alcohol, or other addictions. We will survive with the pain being part of our journey. We will be free to move forward having learned from both the pain and forgiveness. We cannot allow fear to keep us from our journey. If we do not move forward, this is where our journey really stops. We are not free to move forward or to allow beautiful things into our lives. We cannot grow and mature while holding onto the pain. This is especially important given the number of hurting people in our society. The odds are high that people will pass the pain on which they have not dealt with properly. The problem may have more to do with the person causing the pain than the person who was hurt. The person inflicting the pain has difficulty managing their life in a godly manner. When we dare to face the pain, we will be shocked that the fear was only in our minds. The pain is like any bully: when you stand up to it, it is gone. There is freedom and even surprise that it wasn't as bad as we thought. Our minds create and replay our pain, but once it is dealt with properly, the pain passes.

We have talked a lot about forgiving someone who has hurt us. Let us look at the other side. If we have hurt someone, it may go a long way in healing both parties when we apologize. It can close wounds and allow the healing process to begin. We are all born into a world of sin, and we have all sinned. The healing occurs when we are genuinely sorry for our sin and turn away from sin. We can be remorseful for the pain that our choices have caused someone else and apologize. We all need to stop inflicting pain on each other and have genuine remorse. We should never allow fear of rejection to prevent us from apologizing. Fear is never from God, and it holds us captive. When we apologize, we can only do it from the heart and hope that it is received. If they are not at a point where they can accept our apology, then we have still attempted to make peace. A great place to start is to acknowledge their pain and to apologize. It shows them that they matter and that their feelings are important. We do not even have to agree with their version of events. We do not have to agree on who was right or who was wrong. We do not have to agree with who did what to whom. We are merely acknowledging that in some way we caused them pain and that we are sorry for their suffering. When we go further and try to prove our point or that we were right, we often get off course and into causing more pain. We may both have valid arguments, and we may have both said hurtful things. There are always different views because we see things from our own perspectives. Each person may be correct in their interpretation, and both sides can have elements of truth. There is no wrong or right; there is only love and forgiveness.

I am reminded of when Jesus fed the five thousand, it is an example that man could not do this but that with God all things are possible. We may not be able to forgive by our own strength. When we humble ourselves and forgive when we don't want to forgive, there will be healing. It may take time for some wounds to heal and they may even be reopened. Understanding that the pain was inflicted by a person who is wounded and lost helps to understand the pain. It never justifies our pain but will allow us to receive the lesson and enable maturity.

It appears that people hurt one another both by accident and also intentionally. It makes no sense why anyone would intentionally hurt other people. People often hurt loved ones and their own families. Sins are like ripples in the water. A lie, lust, or greed may start out small, and you may think it doesn't matter. Then something happens, and more people get hurt or caught up in the sin. Damage ripples out to your family or someone innocent that you did not mean to hurt. We must stop allowing these ripples to destroy one another. In thinking of a stadium, I am reminded of the wave. Each person stands and waves their arms all around the stadium. We must become the wave for God. We must decide to follow the scriptures and love one another. We are on the same team. It makes no sense to attack and destroy one another.

Christian Support

Being a Christian, we walk in peace and love. We will meet many worldly people who are willing to take advantage of our kind spirit. Keep in mind that worldly people can be selfish and manipulative. Being a Christian does not mean that we are weak or to be abused.

On the contrary, we are strong and compassionate and should not allow ourselves to be abused by worldly people. If we see that a worldly person does not appreciate our help, we can find a person who will improve with our help. Do not waste God's resources on selfish people who at this time have no interest in changing. We have many worldly people around us, and we need to discern whom we can actually help. We must walk in peace and love and not criticize or judge. When we try to help people, we will know by their actions if we will be able to help them. Notice that I said actions and not words in the last sentence. People can have manipulative minds and can say anything to keep us engaged. If we are giving help but do not see any evidence of their life improving, we are not able to help. We can pray for these people and love them, but we cannot make them change. It is ultimately their job to do the work and have a relationship with God to improve their lives. Sometimes it hinders them if we do the work for them. They are not learning the lessons because they are not doing the work. We must remember to empower rather than enable people. If we allow them to use or abuse us, everyone loses. They are not maturing, and we are exhausted. Remember that even when we stop enabling, we are doing this out of love. We can only control our beliefs and actions and cannot pass judgment. We must decide if we are assisting or enabling. We choose our actions and support; we should not allow manipulation. We may love someone deeply, but allowing them to use or abuse us is not helping their situation.

We believe that we have to either deny the pain or we have to let the pain out. We may get to the point where we are able to talk or cry it out. Even if we believe that we get the pain out, it is truly never gone although we temporarily feel better. Accepting the pain as part of our journey enables us to mature as a Christian. Ultimately, we may have to allow the pain in and acknowledge and accept it. Many people are in pain and often inflict their pain on innocent people. We are not able to change the past, but we can acknowledge the pain. Pain will not be denied, and it will express itself in some form. If we recognize that wounded people hurt us and we accept the pain, we will not pass it on to others. Many people try to deny or escape the pain, but it is an illusion. Pain is like energy and must be absorbed to dissipate. If we inflict less pain on one another, there will be wholeness and fewer damaged people in the world. It is imperative that we learn to love one another and stop the pain and suffering.

Worldly or Godly Love

We must understand that there is a difference between worldly love and godly love. I will explain worldly love first. Worldly love is very shallow; it cannot be deep because it takes real work and time to get depth in a relationship. Worldly love is often based on attraction and lust. Attraction and lust are immediate responses and have nothing to do with getting to know a person genuinely. Many times, worldly love is formed in manipulation. Remember we have been brought up in a society that prizes money and things. When we meet someone, the first question is usually "What do you do or what is your job?" Translation: "How much money do you make?" Are you starting to see the shallowness from the very beginning? The moment we meet, we are worrying about our shortcomings and trying to see if the other person will discover them or fill them. Worldly love has to do with me, me, me. Worldly love probably shouldn't be called love at all, but since the purpose of this chapter is to understand love, it will be used in that sense.

The reason that worldly love can't be love is that our hearts have hardened due to the selfishness. What we call love usually only defines how another person makes us feel. For a while, the other person gives us a sense of happiness and hope of filling the emptiness that we feel inside. The attention that they give us makes us feel worthy and valued. Again, this is selfish love with selfish motives. It is not real love; it is a worldly concept of love. We fall prey to this so easily because we have pain and suffering and seek to find a way to be fulfilled. The problem with this worldly idea of love is that it is an illusion. You may wonder at this point if it is possible to meet someone and have a loving, trusting relationship. It is possible, but it takes time to get to know a person's real character, and it takes hard work to develop a loving relationship.

1 Corinthians 13:4–13:7

Love is patient, love is kind. It does not envy, it does not boast, it is not proud. It does not dishonor others, it is not self-seeking, it is not easily angered, it keeps no record of wrongs. Love does not delight in evil but rejoices with the truth. It always protects, always trusts, always hopes, always perseveres.

Godly love is real and has a genuine concern for others. It is not an illusion like worldly love. It is not self-seeking; instead, it is genuine and caring. It is truthful, honest, and mature. Love is patient and kind and puts others' interests above our own. We should have patience with each other and be kind to one another. We are all on a journey to mature and develop as individuals, couples, and families. What we are failing to see is that we are also evolving as a society. What we learn and teach our children shapes the world that they will inherit. We are so used to everything being fast that we have a mindset that everything should be fast and easy. Perhaps the world is moving too fast for us. We have developed the mind to solve problems without developing a moral compass. Our world has evolved, but we are paying the ultimate price for convenience. We have lost the joy in life. We have failed to love each other or to teach our children anything other than the value of a dollar.

I hope you can see that this has damaged every area of our lives including the ability to love one another. You may wonder what I can do? If the problem exists within the entire world and everyone has gone along with this, what difference can I make? This book is designed to strengthen and mature Christians. It is not about being helpless. You are a light, and the only way that the darkness continues is if we do not turn on the lights. We as Christians cannot turn away from this any longer. We must read our Bible and increase our prayers and lean into this intentionally. This we must do on purpose by choice, living our lives with courage. Every one of you may be looking for the one big thing that is the purpose of your life. You should not be looking for the purpose of "your life." Seek God's purpose and further God's will. Become love. Become truth. Become hope. Become light. Right where you are in your home with your family, be loving, truthful, and hopeful; turn on the light. No longer settling for the things that have been accepted by this world. Read your Bible and learn what work needs to be done to change.

Sometimes scriptures will be confusing, and you may read something in one place and feel like it tells you something else in a different verse or chapter. Do not let that stop you in your tracks. Everything was written for a reason. Everything will not apply to every situation. The best advice that I can give you is to trust your motives. When I come to a problem, I look at my motives. What am I pursuing, and why? Let me give you an example. In my place of employment, many managers were manipulative and did things that were not ethical. For several years, I prayed for God to guide me and to survive the day. Things progressed over a period of three years. I finally spoke up and asked a question about overtime, and I was on the company's radar. I will not disclose all that I suffered working for this company. I had gone to every level of management begging for help. There was never anyone who was honest or willing to help me. The stress eventually led to a back injury, and I had no choice but to defend myself. Through the entire process, I prayed about it and watched my motives. I genuinely believe they did not understand how their actions created this environment for me and others. My motives were to teach them that their actions were dishonest and to try to protect other employees. I truly wanted to show them a godly way of doing business instead of their path of deception. It was a difficult situation for me, but it came down to standing up to the corruption. I dealt honestly and truthfully and exhausted any and all avenues and had to stand against the corruption. You can be a Christian who is not doing anything wrong, and the world still attacks. I do not let it put hatred in my heart because they do not understand what they are doing. I try to defend myself against the attacks, and at the same time, I feel sorry for them because they have so much greed and deception in their hearts.

The point is, I did not want to act out of vengeance or hatred, or even worse be motivated by greed. I had to examine my motives many times through this entire period. Initially, I was hurt, angry, and confused. I just continued and watched my motives. I wanted to teach them to take moral responsibility for their decisions. I wanted to create a better work environment for all employees. It came to a point where I just believed that Christians need to take a stand against the evil and corruption. Many Christians are working in very corrupt environments and know precisely what I am talking about. I can only tell you to trust the Holy Spirit to guide you through your daily trials. Always tell the truth and treat people with honesty and integrity. There is pressure to manipulate the truth for money and power. I caution you again to look at your motives. The world is corrupt, but we must find a way to function in a godly way if we are calling ourselves Christians. The world loves to see people calling themselves Christians and doing ungodly things for money or power.

Luke 16:13

No one can serve two masters. Either you will hate the one and love the other, or you will be devoted to one and despise the other. You cannot serve both God and money.

I will be the first to tell you that it is difficult to be a Christian in a world so full of corruption. I cannot tell you what to do in your personal situation. It is always a personal choice between you and God. You need to decide whether you will contribute to the corruption or choose to do what is ethical and honest. Remember that difficult situations and hardships purify our souls and reveal our real character and motives.

My grandsons were telling me a story about someone lying about their age to gain access to an event for free. They asked me what I would do in this case. I told them I would have paid the entrance fee for the twelve-year-old child. They said, "Why no one would know." I answered, "Where do you draw the line? If you compromise your ethics this time, what will you stop at next time?" They were quiet and thought about it. I was planting seeds that day. Let's get serious is it really harder to do the right thing? Do we think for a moment it is easier to do something wrong or unjust? Do we really believe that we harm no one when we do something wrong or deceitful? There is always a victim! That is one of the great deceptions: no one will know. We know, and God knows. Every time we compromise our ethics, we move the line, and the edges get a little blurrier. Every time we fail to do what is right or ethical because we are afraid to do what is right, we allow fear to make our decision. Our fear or lack of ethics change the world. We pass the pain and deception on to someone. We go home to our families as mothers or fathers, and we think we leave our work lives at work. The truth is that we are who we are. If we are dishonest in any part of our life, it shows up in all of our life. It is time we all stop accepting worldly standards as normal. What we accept we also allow. What we allow, we also become. Tell our children and grandchildren that all those compromises and unethical decisions hurt no one. Tell them that no one would know. Look at the legal system we have left them; there is no justice, only manipulation. Most laws are so unbalanced that truth cannot be seen in them. Who we are and how we conduct ourselves matters in this world. It matters what we teach our children and grandchildren. It matters how we conduct our business. It matters who we are individually because that is who we become collectively. It matters!

Galatians 5:14–5:15

For the entire law is fulfilled in keeping this one command: "Love your neighbor as yourself." If you bite and devour each other, watch out, or you will be destroyed by each other.

There are no clear answers for every situation. People and life events can have many dimensions. The important thing is not to allow our minds to manipulate the truth. There is a clear distinction between right and wrong. Often our minds try to negotiate or justify our choices. Our minds are corrupted by the world. Trust your spirit to guide you and always examine your motives. It will give you a clear view of what you are choosing and why. Life will throw curves at us, and a difficult decision will be inevitable. When we know who we are and where we stand, the decisions get easier. Many of us are so lost because we have let the world define us. We have compromised our morals and ethics so many times that we no longer know who we are or what we believe. I can tell you that people are not perfect. We are human and wounded and damaged. People that we love will hurt and deceive us. We need to remember when they do, they are coming from a place of pain and damage. The world that we have created is selfish and manipulative. If we had only held to the command to love one another, the world could have been caring, loving, and honest. When we seek to satisfy the needs of just me, me, me, we destroy us, us, us. We have taken life beyond survival to greed, excess, and manipulation.

To repent means to have sincere remorse and regret for what we have done and to turn away from it. It changes accepting what we have done as normal to unacceptable and not continuing in the behavior. It is being sorry for the pain that we inflicted on someone else for a selfish or unjust reason. Many people in the world are filled with pain, and they can't let go because no one has ever said they were sorry. Humbling ourselves to acknowledge their pain is a beautiful gift to both the person in pain and the person who caused the pain. Sometimes we don't say that we are sorry because we are afraid of how the person will react. We cannot predict how another person will react when they are in pain. We can only give the gift of an apology. If they accept the apology immediately, you can both move forward. Both parties are released from the pain and know a little more about each other. If they reject it immediately, then you offered, but they chose to hold on to their pain. The injured party may not be ready to let go of the pain at this time. If they never forgive you, you at least cared about them and made a sincere effort towards healing.

Romans 5:8

But God demonstrates his own love for us in this;
While we were still sinners, Christ died for us.

I have had several situations in my life that required
that I forgive someone who had hurt me deeply. It
was not my own actions but their actions and choices
that caused the pain. I had to forgive them because
God forgave me while I was a sinner. I also had to
realize that they did not have a Christian mindset and
did not understand what they were doing. When we
can move past the idea of being right or winning, we
move toward mutual love. There is so much growth
in forgiving someone who did not apologize. It is our
choice to forgive them whether they are sorry or not.
We can choose to forgive them and release ourselves
from the pain. We do not have to wait for them to
apologize or realize that they caused severe pain. The
truth is that some people are not capable of understanding that they did something wrong or inflicted
needless pain on others. If we wait for them to decide
when forgiveness occurs, it may never happen. It is
a powerful choice to forgive someone. Choosing to
move forward free from the pain is power. Don't let
others decide how long you stay in a hurtful situation
or wait on an apology.

Luke 23:34

Jesus said "Father, forgive them, for they do not know what they are doing." And they divided up his clothes by casting lots.

It is hard to forgive someone who has never admitted what they did or said that they were sorry. It is not impossible to overcome these situations. I can give you an example from my life. I felt that God wanted me to forgive someone who had hurt me very deeply and betrayed a close bond. I told God that I could not forgive this person because they were not sorry. This went on for several years. Finally, I felt that I should write a letter stating that I would forgive this person. I felt God guided me to write a simple letter of forgiveness. The letter could have no ulterior motives or any manipulation. That is exactly what I wrote: a letter of forgiveness. I mailed the letter and was obedient to God. I never received a response to my letter. The point is that I did not need a response. I was set free from the pain of the situation just by the act of obedience in writing the letter. I can tell you that many of my life experiences have been filled with pain and heartache. Accepting these experiences and letting them teach me instead of allowing them to stop me has been an amazing journey. I have discovered a deeper love, more tolerance, and a real desire to care and teach. The world is full of injustice. We need to realize that life is not going to be fair as long as humans do not love one another. Justice and honesty are very rare in our society. We all need to stop following the world and be a light exactly where we are in the world. Stop looking for the big thing that you are supposed to do. God needs us right where we are. There is some goodness in all of us. Many people have their goodness buried under so much pain. We cannot fix the world overnight, and it will take work. We can begin by doing what is right and godly and to love one another. This book is about calling people who have a love for God but are still operating in a worldly way. We have not been able to understand how to function in a corrupt world and serve God. Our roots and commitment are weak. I am reminded of the parable of the seeds that Jesus taught.

Matthew 13:3–13:8

Then he told them many things in parables, saying: "A farmer went out to sow his seed. As he was scattering the seed, some fell along the path, and birds came and ate it up. Some fell on rocky places, where it did not have much soil. It sprang up quickly, because the soil was shallow. But when the sun came up, the plants were scorched, and they withered because they had no root. Other seed fell among the thorns, which grew up and chocked the plants. Still other seed fell on good soil, where it produced a crop-a hundred, sixty or thirty times what was sown."

Many Christians do believe, and they love God, but they are not on good soil and have not developed roots. We need to stop allowing the thorns to prevent us from growing and maturing. We may wonder how to get on good soil and establish roots. Begin by understanding the pain and suffering in the world. Commit ourselves to not being part of the corruption. Take a stand for God and understand his word by reading it and following the example of Jesus Christ. Every lesson in the Bible keeps us from falling into a trap or into deception. Another example would be to freely give. When Mathew was sending out his twelve disciples, one of his instructions to them was to give freely.

Matthew 10:8

Heal the sick, raise the dead, cleanse those who have leprosy, drive out demons. Freely you have received; freely give.

The reason that we must give freely is that if it is not freely given, it has ulterior motives and manipulation. We must do good things and give freely out of love while not seeking anything for ourselves. Let me give you an example to let you know how important it is to watch your motives. There is a man who provides very well financially for his family, and his wife is able to stay at home with the children. On the surface, it sounds great and is appreciated. Part of the reason that he does not want her to work to work is control.

He enjoys having final say on anything she spends. He gives with one hand and takes back with the other. For his wife, this creates feelings of both thankfulness and resentment. If he had financially provided with a giving heart and then treated her as an equal on decisions, she would have felt valued. When you do something for someone, look at your motives. Do things out of love; do not let manipulation be your motive. Only true, sincere love lasts; manipulation and motives will always be exposed. There is a reason why Jesus gave us the command to love one another. When we love one another, we are unable to harm or inflict pain on each other. When godly love exists in our hearts, we are unable to lie or deceive others. This is why we must understand the difference between worldly love and godly love. Worldly love is self-serving and manipulative. Godly love is sincere and has a deep love and compassion for others. We need to have godly love in our relationship with God. We need a godly love for Jesus and for one another. We must understand the difference, because worldly love is not real love.

Chapter 7

Perseverance

It seems that many people are not honest in this day and age. There was a time when deals were made with a handshake. It was a time when many people were as good as their word. I feel extreme sorrow for the generations that may never know a more honest world. People today are being pushed to a breaking point because of corruption, deception, greed, and selfishness. This is the world that we created and inherited. You will see that I have used some examples many times in multiple chapters. This is not by accident but instead by perseverance. It is important to explain the how and why that has caused our world to be what it is today. I am determined to help people understand the importance of their choices and to drive many points home again and again.

The meaning of *perseverance* according to the Free Dictionary is "steady persistence in adhering to a course of action, a belief or a purpose. Steadfastness."

There are going to be difficult times. There is no doubt about the difficulties in this world. The question remains: What will you do? Do you roll up in a ball and suffer? Do you join in harming and manipulating for self-preservation? Do you turn to drugs or alcohol? Do you say "Enough!" and dig in and take a stand as a Christian? Only you can make your decision. No matter what you choose, life will be difficult. The real question is "How do you want to live your life?" Will you be a person who contributed or allowed the corruption? Will you stand and have deep roots and defend your right to live as a Christian refusing to go along with the corruption of this world?

We have all seen the way many people calling themselves Christians represent themselves in the world. I am not suggesting that you go to work on Monday morning demanding things change. I am not telling you to go into the office and try to save everyone. Worldly people are not ready to receive any message this way. What I am suggesting is that you begin to study your Bible. You can turn away from wrongdoing and allow yourself to get some strong roots. Don't participate in the office gossip and be aware of the choices that you make. Be mindful of who you have become in this world. Start with yourself and then move on to help your family and social circle. In the end, it is a personal choice for everyone. We cannot force our opinion on anyone. They may not be in a position to see what we see, hear what we hear or feel what we feel. We lead by example by being honest and trustworthy. To be a Christian, we need a strong foundation. A stronger prayer life, a specific time to read the Bible, and a more ethical social group are all improvements.

Luke 10:23–10:24

Then he turned to his disciples and said privately, "Blessed are the eyes that see what you see. For I tell you that many prophets and kings wanted to see what you see but did not see it, and to hear what you hear but did not hear it."

The point is, we must not to give up because it matters to all humanity. We can change and choose a different path. Often, we keep repeating the same experience in life because we do not know what else is possible. We accept worldly actions as normal behavior. We can change, but it will require determination and effort. We all need to be conscious of our choices. We need to take our mind off of auto pilot and be mindful of our choices. We need to be aware of where our decisions will lead us and others. To be conscious of our choices means to be aware or awake when making them. Maybe at this point, you are sick of the shallowness, greed, and manipulation that floods our world. Perhaps it is time to admit that it is not working for any of us. It is actually making all of us miserable.

When we see where that road has led us, it is time to admit that we have taken a wrong turn.

Before any of us are truly ready for a battle, we need to put on the whole armor of God. We need to mature and develop godly character. Understanding where humanity made a wrong turn is important, but we must also stay away from worldliness. It is not enough to realize how humanity lost its way collectively but to be committed to making godly choices in our everyday lives. These small daily choices will add up to change and a significant movement. When we stay on the path following Jesus, we will see eternal change for many people. We must understand this is a lifestyle change that needs to be maintained. It requires us to maintain our relationship with God. It requires us to seek godly knowledge. Like any relationship worthwhile it requires effort and faithfulness.

James 1:2–1:4

Consider it pure joy, my brothers and sisters, whenever you face trials of many kinds, because you know that the testing of your faith produces perseverance. Let perseverance finish its work so that you may be mature and complete, not lacking anything.

How many opportunities are we missing in our lives because of selfishness? We will miss the opportunity to know God with a pure heart. We will miss the opportunity to follow Jesus. We will miss the chance to truly

love other people. When we make life all about ourselves, we miss that it is about seeking a relationship
with God. Compare the difference between our small
selfish plan and God's plan of love and peace. There is
no comparison. We are not just missing opportunities
for ourselves. We are also damaging the lives of other
people. We cannot love our loved ones deeply because
worldly love is shallow. We manipulate family and
friends because we are all that matters. If we think our
selfishness hurts no one, think again. We cannot count
the number of people who get hurt when we live our
lives selfishly. Selfishness damages and poisons every
relationship in our lives. It changes who we are with
our parents because we view our parents for what
they can do for us. We should instead appreciate the
incredible gift of a loving parent. Selfishness requires
that our parents support anything we desire and
gives very little in return. How can we offer anything
in return when we only consider our needs? Our relationship with a spouse will also be toxic when we are
selfish. When we are selfish, we are unable to comprehend that other people have feelings. Selfish people
view partners only for what they can do to meet their
needs. They may go from one relationship to the next
as partners get exhausted trying to fill the selfish person's needs while their own needs are sacrificed. As
a sibling, our selfishness damages relationships and
keeps real love from blooming. Even if our siblings
love us, they do not feel loved by us when we are
selfish. People used and abused by selfish people feel

used and abused. As a parent, selfishness is the most dangerous because it teaches children how to relate to this world. Selfishness teaches children manipulation and to seek only selfish desires. Selfishness does not teach children how to love others or about self-sacrifice. Children are precious gifts and need to be raised to have compassion for other people. When children learn only selfishness, it leaves them damaged and emotionally bankrupt. A selfish parent can harm a child through their entire life. We must remember balance as a parent and create a safe, loving environment for children to develop.

I am attempting to get you to see the importance of loving one another as in the previous chapter. The reason that it is so important is that without sincere love, there can be no real change. Perseverance is essential because we need to be committed to change and to work continuously. We have the power to do the work and to be what God intended. Our power has gotten lost among all the problems in the world. Our power lies within us; it is the Holy Spirit and our faith in God and his Son Jesus Christ. Our faith is so important, but actions are also required.

James 2:24

You see that a person is considered righteous by what they do and not by faith alone.

Having faith in God is a good start, but there is much more required. Jesus came to teach us much more than just to believe. It is sad to say, but even the corruption in man's mind can get tangled in religion. This is why we are instructed to only follow teachings acknowledging Jesus Christ as our Lord and Savior. Humankind has corrupted everything in the world. God knows who are his and tells us to follow biblical teachings. Do not be mistaken, Christians have courage and strength. Our strength comes from God, and our understanding comes from the scriptures. The reason that we may feel weak is that we are not getting our faith recharged daily through prayer and Bible study. We need time for both of these because we cannot grow and mature on our own. When we consider the percentage of worldliness and the percentage of God that we get daily, we can understand why we feel overwhelmed. We are continually dealing with worldly problems to the point of exhaustion. We are so overwhelmed that we fail to take the time to seek God. Since understanding how to overcome the world lies in the scriptures and following Jesus, we must make the time. It comes down to commitment and perseverance. These struggles will not go away or be resolved until we understand how to overcome the problems. We can continue blindly in our suffering, or we can find the godly instructions that can actually guide us through the issues. Following Jesus is not just about saving ourselves and spending an eternity in heaven. Following Jesus is so much more important than just saving ourselves. We have an opportunity to grow to become the mature body of Christ and to love God and each other. The good news is that when we put God first in our life, and we accept Jesus as our Lord and Savior, we will be filled with the Holy Spirit. The battles and trials of this world will still come, but now we have an ally. The Holy Spirit will help us to understand and endure all the hardships and trials. We can allow and learn from the pain growing to maturity as Christians. From there we learn to follow the examples of Jesus Christ.

Romans 5:3–5:4

Not only so, but we also glory in our sufferings, because we know that suffering produces perseverance; perseverance, character; and character, hope.

We need to terminate the idea that life is fair and that it should be easy. Life could have been fair, and it could have been easy if we had followed the command to love one another. Most human beings have failed to follow that command. We live in an unfair and increasingly difficult world. We all suffer because we are reaping what we have sown. We must stop expecting it to be any different. The sooner we accept the reality of the situation and understand the impact, the sooner we make changes.

You may feel successful because you have an expensive home, a powerful job, a luxury car and or an attractive spouse. These are worldly standards that you are using to measure success. By godly standards, did you put God first? Did you love one another? Did you harm anyone to get your job or your possessions? Were you honest and truthful? Did you help a brother or sister? Did you teach your children well? Were you an example that you would want people to follow? Do not be deceived by the definition of success. Our choices have powerful consequences. They literally define the entire world. With the internet and cell phones, we instantly influence each other and the world. Misleading movies show us how others have perfect lives. We see actors being successful and happy in movie after movie. The message is that if we have all these worldly desires that we will live happily ever after. We have bought into the illusion of fame and fortune. It promises us things that it cannot deliver. We are trying to live a fantasy and an illusion. It robs us from all the real joy in our lives. What is wrong with being an honest person and enjoying our lives? We all must admit that the fantasies that we see on television are nothing like real life. It creates suffering to believe that other people have wonderful lives while the real world is unfair and unjust. Living in a fantasy keeps us from dealing with the reality of the world. When we go from fantasy to being unfulfilled by reality, it makes life unbearable. The proof that beauty, wealth and fame are illusions is revealed with the journey. As we get older we all age so, therefore, beauty fails. Wealth cannot be taken with us when we die, so it too is an illusion. Money only makes us worldly happy while we are alive.

In most cases, it causes more problems than it solves. Most people view wealth selfishly and try to accumulate more and more. There seems to be no amount that really makes them happy. Today, fame appears to be possible for average people because of reality shows. The odds are near zero, but young people feel a parallel with the reality stars and believe it is possible. Fame also fails because it is fleeting. Very few ever get their fifteen seconds of fame, and even fewer have a long career. The youth of today want everything instantly and feel entitled to everything. They do not want to work for anything. Most have selfish ambitions and lack work ethics. In defense of our youth, they are what we have made them. I am not attacking our youth, on the contrary, I am hoping that parents and grandparents put in the work to guide and nurture our youth. It is not too late to contribute to their lives.

It amazes me that the more we try to be "civilized," the more uncivilized we become. We use our modern devices as weapons to hurt each other. Look at the internet; some people use it to post horrible things about others. Predators use it to find victims to abuse. Television airs real murders and attacks for entertainment. People abuse drugs and alcohol to escape the pain of civilization. Mankind develops more deadly weapons for warfare. Cameras have to be mounted everywhere, including homes. People have become more dangerous and violent because they are unable to handle the stress and pain of the world. I do not believe that this was God's plan for us. We have to take full ownership of this so-called civilization. We are at a critical point in the world. It is time to wake up. Perhaps we can find ways to slow our world down. We can turn off the devices and make time for God. We can work fewer hours and spend more time sowing into our children. We can want less and find happiness in what we have been given. Instead of watching television shows that are negative, we can do something positive. Begin to pay attention to what your life includes. Make choices to only allow things in your life that build and protect you and your family. Do not focus on how overwhelming it is when you look at the problems of humanity. It can seem hopeless and overwhelming. Focus all your energy and strength on correcting yourself and then your family. Once you get a clear vision, then you can reach to help someone else. Get yourself stable before trying to save anyone else. The real power for this is keeping the command to love one another.

When I speak of perseverance, it is through years of suffering, growing, and maturing. God has been working with me for decades. I know that if I had not cooperated with God and tried to understand his teachings that I would not have matured. At the same time, if I had not been under constant pressure and attack, I would not have learned perseverance. What I am attempting to share with you in this book is a clearer path. I am hoping to share things that it has taken me years to learn and understand. I am hoping that it will help you to accept pain and suffering and allow you to move forward with a renewed faith and hope. My hope is that understanding why we are hurting one another instead of loving one another changes our course. The real desire of this book is to help you understand why we are in pain and how to move forward to healing and love.

James 1:12–1:15

Blessed is the one who perseveres under trial because, having stood the test, that person will receive the crown of life that the Lord has promised to those who love him. When tempted, no one should say, "God is tempting me." For God cannot be tempted by evil, nor does he tempt anyone; but each person is tempted when they are dragged away by their own evil desires and enticed. Then, after desire has conceived, it gives birth to sin; and sin, when full-grown, gives birth to death.

This scripture explains how sin develops in our lives. There first must be an evil desire within us. We have discussed the many places that these evil desires can be suggested to us through the media and internet and from other people. After we begin to desire something and being enticed by it, we think about it constantly. We then act on our thoughts and desire is conceived and gives birth to sin. When sin is full grown, it gives birth to death. People need to realize that when we have evil thoughts, we must stop the process at that point. Our minds can keep thinking about the desire because it leads us into action. We foolishly follow ungodly desires and give into sin. Even if it appears that no one knows and that we may get by with it for a period of time, it is an illusion. At some point, the sin will be exposed, and many lives will be damaged. As mentioned in the scripture above, God does not tempt anyone. Any evil desire is not coming from God, and we must be aware of temptation and turn away. Our minds can be led astray and easily tempted. We must have a godly knowledge and strong morals to turn away. It should help all of us if we can recognize where sin originates. Most of my life I did not understand how or why sin developed. I did not recognize the traps or deception. Sin and temptation are not from God. I always tried to make good choices but really could not understand why people did what they did or why the world was the way it was. We need to be aware of things enticing us such as greed, power or lust to name a few. Often, we make everyday choices without considering our motives or the consequences. We never even consider whether it is right or wrong or if it will harm someone else. This often occurs in our business or work life. Unfortunately, so many businesses require us to do unethical things that we no longer question them. We accept what we are doing as reasonable and appropriate by worldly standards. Even if the decisions we are making causes us to feel that something may be wrong or unethical. We quickly dismiss those feelings by saying that it is business. Instead of dismissing those feelings as business, we need to be aware of those feelings. Every choice that we make defines our world and can compromise our ethics. Instead of automatically saying it is just business, look at who is hurt by unethical decisions. There is always a victim in doing something wrong or immoral. There are many unethical practices in the business world. They intentionally manipulate and deceive for profit. It is their standard practice. Manipulation and deceit are often automatic and accepted as normal. There is no resistance to their deception, and corruption is encouraged. If there is no resistance, then there is no boundary to stop its spread. That is a frightening thought because we do not know how much worse things will get if there is nothing to stop the corruption.

The success of a person or group to deceive an individual depends on them isolating us. The bad news is that they are masters of deception. They know the deceptive laws and maneuvers well. They continue to get by with it because they operate in darkness and where there is no one to defend us. We all need to shine a light on the wrongdoings of individuals and corporations. The truth is that if we unite and shine a light and protect each other, we can change things. An example that I can give is a long-term disability provider. When they accept the premiums from all the workers, there is no problem. If a worker then becomes disabled, they do everything in their power to keep from paying and honoring their contract. The reason that they get away with this is that the disabled person is isolated. We do not know how the system works. We are isolated, and the others paying premiums have no idea what will happen if they need this benefit.

Another example, our government has an agency to handle injured workers. An injured worker fills out paperwork regarding an injury. The corrupt employer has had numerous injuries before and knows how to manipulate the system. They begin the manipulation the day of the injury and continue throughout the entire process. They have no ethics, and the system is designed in favor of the corporation because of money. They will pay corrupt doctors who only care about money. Being naive to the system one would believe that doctors have a code of ethics to first do no harm. There are a few doctors who will lie about a patient's condition for money or profit, but they are rare. The companies have personal relationships with these unethical doctors. Most doctors genuinely do care about their patients and want them to recover. I do not wish to dishonor physicians by associating them with the Independent Medical Examiners used by unethical employers.

Amos 5:12

For I know how many are your offenses and how great your sins. You oppress the righteous and take bribes, and you deprive the poor of justice in the courts.

The point is that these abuses are allowed and practiced every day in this country. We are governed by laws that are corrupt. Lawmakers have the delusion that they are making the country stronger by creating laws that favor industry. Lawmakers believe that it makes sense to keep corporations producing and protect them no matter what crimes they commit against humanity. They have instead created a perfect storm. They have created an environment where workers are disposable and can be treated unjustly. They have managers and owners that will do anything for money. It has created working environments that are very hostile for workers. Humans attack humans for money and use their power to abuse workers.

Ephesians 5:11–5:13

Have nothing to do with fruitless deeds of darkness, but rather expose them. It is shameful to even mention what the disobedient do in secret. But everything exposed by the light becomes visible-and everything that is illuminated becomes a light.

What kind of future does that leave our children and grandchildren? Lawmakers were misguided by greed and power and made many decisions to tip the scales in favor of the wealthy manufactures and businesses. It is no wonder that corruption is so extreme in almost every business in the United States and possibly worldwide. They have not been taught ethics and have no morals. It is considered necessary to win by any means, no matter whom they hurt. We are governed by corrupt leaders and laws. *Any time you tip the scale for any reason, you create an imbalance.* They have created injustice for us all. When cases are judged individually with no prior imbalance, we can get close to justice. The more we stand together, the more significant the change. Unfortunately, we have to deal with the world in which we have been born. We do not have the luxury of justice or honesty. Often, we are victimized by an unjust world. Regardless of the state of the world, we must still persevere. We have a calling to become mature Christians and to put on the full armor of God. We must throw off everything that hinders and the sin that entangles us. Strong and mature Christians are vital to this world. We must never grow weary or have a weak heart.

Hebrews 12:1–12:3

Therefore, since we are surrounded by such a great cloud of witnesses, let us throw off everything that hinders and the sin that so easily entangles. And let us run with perseverance the race marked out for us, fixing our eyes on Jesus, the pioneer and perfecter of faith. For the joy set before him, he endured the cross, scorning its shame, and sat down at the right hand of the throne of God. Consider him who endured such opposition from sinners, so that you will not grow weary and lose heart.

This scripture tells us not to grow weary or to lose heart when we run into opposition from sinners. We have no choice but to deal with the world and all its corruption. The way we deal with it must be to see the ungodly decisions that the world is making and to be prepared with godliness. There is no other answer, and understanding the scriptures provides us with everything that we need to overcome the world. It may help to study the examples that Jesus taught in the New Testament. Christians need to be prepared to see the traps and trials that we are facing. When Christians stand in their faith, they can make a difference in the world. We cannot grow weary because the battle is not finished. We cannot lose heart because we now know that we must dig deeper and get strong roots. Jesus endured the cross for us and is now sitting down at the right hand of God. Growing as the mature body of Christ requires us to get over our selfishness and to do the hard work. The world has been self-indulgent and shallow for a very long time. It is time for Christians to do the real work and to develop godly character and determination. We as Christians are to fix our eyes on Jesus, the pioneer and perfecter of faith.

Chapter 8

A Parent's Purpose

This chapter is dedicated to the children because they are the next generation. They are the innocents inheriting the mess that we have created. It is also where we can begin to plant seeds of hope, truth, and love.

Parents always say that children do not come with a manual or instruction book. While I don't have a degree in raising children, I do have thirty-eight years of experience. I also have fifteen years of experience being a grandmother. I may be able to share my life experiences and shed light on what should be in that manual.

Worldly Parenting

Let's begin by talking about the worldly or standard ways that children are being raised today. Parents believe that their job is to feed, clothe, and take the child to school or daycare. We also keep them continuously entertained through television, movies, games, and internet. We buy them toys and candy, and generally spoil children. Some parents work but still find time for their child's sporting events. We also take them to the doctor for medical attention. Sounds pretty normal, right? Have you ever seen so many children on ADHD/ADD medication? Have you ever seen so many spoiled and entitled children? We may think that we are good parents by the world's standards. When we entertain children constantly, they lack time to be bored or creative. When we buy them things, we are teaching them to value possessions. It may make the children selfish and unable to connect with others. Children do not learn how to suffer through any disappointment. Worldly parenting does not develop a happy, balanced child. Worldly parenting takes care of the body and the mind. It has completely forgotten about the child's soul and moral compass. Unfortunately, most parents are in extreme pain and suffering in their own lives. All the stress and suffering in the world make it very difficult to have the patience and time needed to raise healthy and happy children. Often parents pass the pain and stress that they cannot handle onto their children.

Godly Parenting

As Godly parents, we must first set a loving and honest example. We need to respect our spouse and develop a loving marriage. Our children will benefit from this strong example. They will feel safe and loved. We must teach them about loving God and to love one another. This will teach them to put God first, and loving others will keep them from being selfish.

Instead of entertaining children via media sources, spend time connecting to them. Teach children the importance of always telling the truth. This will keep manipulation and deception from taking root and will give them morals and ethics. We cannot protect our children from the world so we must prepare them to survive in it. When we send our children to public school, they are getting a worldly education. They are surrounded by worldly children whose parents do not set good examples. The seeds and values that we sow have to be strong enough to last a lifetime. These are not one-time lessons; these principles should be present and reinforced in daily life.

Proverbs 22:6

Train a child in the way he should go, and when he is old he will not turn from it.

This is what is missing in today's society. We are entertained and educated but have no morals or ethics. We teach our children to seek money and careers instead of godly values. Things as simple as honesty and loving one another would be a starting point. Godly changes would occur if parents would read the Bible and really live a Christian life. We will never grow deep roots or be able to change unless we make it a priority. It is more difficult and vital to parent correctly in this day and age. Being a child was simple, and parenting was also simple when the world was more innocent. Today, children are learning things at much earlier ages and have access to very mature images through television and the internet. We did not have to worry about who our child was talking with or who may be trying to lure our child away in the past. Often, children seeking love are lured away. We need to provide a stable, loving home to protect our children. Children are bored so quickly and want constant stimulation. They have not learned how to relax or how to be a child.

We can make Sunday God's day and family day. They will always value this family time. When children have family time, it helps them find their place in the world. Damaging children is our greatest shame. Children are the casualties of generations of sins. The term *casualty* means a person or thing badly affected by an event or situation. Parents are putting careers first, and their children are being raised by strangers. Even if they are cared for properly, they are not receiving the family bonding or love that they need. They are not being taught vital lessons of morals and ethics. Often parents feel guilty and buy children things. This may make the child happy, and the parent feels better for a short period. The long-term effect of this is that the child still did not receive real-time or love from the parent. The child has learned that to get more things, they need to feel bad or misbehave. Children learn manipulation and worldly values. I realize many parents have to work and that it is necessary. I would suggest downsizing or minimizing unnecessary purchases and spending meaningful time developing your child's character and morals. We may think that the traits of honesty and love are merely part of their personality. The truth is that children are born innocent and pure, but the sin of this world does have an effect on and mold them. They are born into sin and need strong morals and ethics to survive. Teach children to be happy and thankful for everything that they have been given. It will teach them gratitude and appreciation instead of always seeking more possessions.

Luke 1:17

And he will go on before the Lord, in the spirit and power of Elijah, to turn the hearts of the parents to their children and the disobedient to the wisdom of the righteous-to make ready a people prepared for the Lord.

You as parents probably did not receive this kind of love and instruction as children. It is difficult to teach what you have not been shown. It is vital that we all dig deep and learn how to instruct and guide innocent children. Pain and neglect can damage a person for a lifetime. The pain that we pass on to children changes them and shapes the next generation. Children may not be able to read or understand the Bible without our help. Buying them a child's Bible and reading it with them is a good idea. It would also be best to study your own adult Bible. This way you will be able to teach them godly principles while they are still young. Life is difficult for children growing up in this world. They need an anchor for their souls and godly principles to guide them. There are so many worldly dangers and traps that they are not prepared to overcome.

Loving the child from a sincere heart is the first step. The second is to be consistent in their lives. We must enforce family rules because they set boundaries. As our children grow and mature, the rules and boundaries change. As parents, teach godly principles such as telling the truth, loving one another and sharing. We must really listen to our children when they speak. Take the time to bend over and look them in the eyes. They will know that you are listening and care about their feelings. Children will feel safe and valued when we do our job well.

When you say no, mean no. Speak to your children firmly without making them feel fear. We must have respect for ourselves as heads of the household. The children will only respond to our instruction with the same commitment as it is given. In other words, enforce the clear instruction, do not backslide on your word. If we waver on our instructions, children will not take them seriously. We must have the character to follow through and to be a leader. Children will learn that we mean what we say and realize we have integrity and authority. When we are unclear on instructions, it creates confusion for children. We have to make boundaries clear and not keep moving the lines so that children clearly understand. We as parents must overcome selfishness and dishonesty to set strong examples. Our real job as a parent is to raise children that are honest, loving and godly and to prepare them for adulthood.

The pain in our lives and the stress of our jobs must never be passed onto our children. We have a horrible legacy in this world of passing our pain and stress onto someone weaker. Often this pain is inflicted onto innocent children. If everyone were honest, they would tell you that they work to buy more things for themselves and their family. That is true, but often we buy extravagant things at the expense of our families. We tell ourselves that we are providing the best for our families. By worldly standards, that is true. By godly standards, it is not true. Our children need love, guidance, morals, and values more than they need a new toy or a bigger house or a second car. We set the example for our children, and we teach them what is acceptable. What examples arc we setting for them? Life is difficult for busy parents, and the last thing you want to hear is that more is added to your busy life. It is not more that you will be adding. It is merely choosing what to pursue in life. It is teaching godly values and setting godly examples instead of teaching worldliness to our children. When we raise our children correctly, they grow up to be a blessing. When we do not put in the work and sow into their lives, they get their values from a corrupt world. Children who have worldly values are damaged and fall into traps. They do not have the skills to handle the pain and suffering. Worldly children grow up shallow and selfish and manipulative. They often turn to drugs and alcohol to ease their pain. It is not their fault; they were merely born into a corrupt world and not taught the skills to deal with the pain. Teaching our children godly values does two things, it will begin to make this world a better place, and it helps them survive the current corruption. We can see how failing to teach our children morals, and ethics has damaged us all. It is vital that we dig in and do the work to save our children.

It is evident that society is dumbfounded by the problems in this world. We only have to look at the prisons. Our law enforcement officers (God Bless Them) are overwhelmed with what they deal with every day. The answer that society has come up with is to incarcerate all the people doing drugs and committing crimes. It makes no sense to me to wait until the end to try to fix the problems. Why do we wait until all these adults have drug problems and commit crimes and then lock them up? Many criminals get out early because they are running out of room. The problem begins long before they are adults. It goes back to teaching morals and ethics to our children and preparing them to make good and godly choices. Many people in our prison systems could have had different lives if only they had been loved, supported and guided. It is not just the children of today that we are failing but everyone that was a child and did not receive what they needed to be whole. Damaged children grow up to be damaged adults.

Fathers

I would encourage you to be strong, honorable leaders of your families. Lead from a strong, godly spirit and always do what is right and honest. You are setting an example for your children. Your wives will be able to respect you. Your experience in this world is based on who you are inside and the choices that you make. Turn away from worldly desires, and desire what God has planned for you. If you want to be respected, respectfully carry yourself. Do not sacrifice your dignity for money, God will provide all that you need. It would be better to have modest things and value your family. Everything you do and everything you say is an example to your children. Do not look at other men in the world for what you should strive to be. Most people are worldly and settle for worldly standards, you are more. You can also become more even if you have settled and failed in the past. Do not hold yourself to worldly standards; strive to hold yourself to godly standards both as a father and a husband. You will never regret this decision. You have no idea how much more you are capable of becoming. If there is anything in your life keeping you from being a loving husband or father, walk away from it now. You can put it down and commit to being so much more.

1 John 1:9

If we confess our sins, he is faithful and just and will forgive us our sins and purify us from all unrighteousness.

As men, husbands, and fathers, you have so much more to offer. You will also have so much more to gain as you begin to do what is right and honest. As you establish a deeper love for God, you will also have a deeper love for your wife and children. You will walk with integrity, peace, and love. Life will become more fulfilling than it was when you walked worldly. There is no rite of passage in this country for men. There is no test or point when you know you have become a man. There are not many examples in our society that define being a man. Most men have been taught to win at any cost. If it costs you your integrity, it costs too much. Since society has failed to set an example, I suggest you follow our example in Jesus Christ. He sacrificed his life for us, he loved us, and he could not lie or do anything unethical. You will never be per-fect, but you will learn so much as you are trying to follow his example. You will make your life and the lives of your family better living this way. You must turn away from the worldly distractions and focus on higher things. Be the kind of man that your wife and children trust and want to follow. Be the kind of man that deserves their respect and loyalty.

Mothers

There are different circumstances in families today. You may be blessed to have a loving and supportive husband and father for your children. You may be married, but the love and support that you need may not be there. You may be single and raising your children alone.

The home where both parents are loving and engaged in the marriage is an ideal environment for the children to flourish. Be careful that you do not measure this by worldly standards. If you use worldly standards, you will have worldly children. You are blessed if you have a loving, faithful marriage. Also, make sure you pursue a faith-filled marriage.

The home where one parent is a Christian and the other is worldly can be very difficult. It may feel like a battlefield for the children. I would encourage you to pray for your spouse. The need is more important to protect the children. Often worldly love is very shallow, and it does not support the stress of life. Children in the middle of this need to be a priority.

Let God guide you and show you how to work out the difficulties in the marriage while being committed to the protection of the children. Put an intentional focus on what examples you are setting for the children. Unfortunately, in this world, all children are not put in homes that are ideal. No matter the circumstances, your job remains the same. You need to protect your children, teach them godly values and love them. This is your priority every day.

In a home where you are a single parent the workload doubles. The best-case scenario is that you can forgive your spouse for the past and put the children first. It can be difficult when you feel wounded or let down by your former partner. Regardless of the pain that came from the breakup, there are children involved. Their safety, welfare and moral guidance must come first. Often, single mothers just look for the next man to fix things. The truth is that you really need to take the time to get to know someone before you expose your children to a stranger. Every time you bring males around your children who are not their biological fathers, the risk of abuse or sexual abuse goes up substantially. It takes time to know a person's motives and character. If he says he is a Christian but does worldly things, he is lying. I know that it is difficult financially and very lonely. Regardless, you have children to protect, and they must be your first priority. Children may need time to adjust and feel safe. When you immediately start dating, you put your needs and desires before those of the children. You need to slow things down and wait to see what kind of character a man has before allowing him into your life and around your children. It should be several months of talking and going on dates before you feel comfortable and know his motives and character. Your children are precious and need to be protected. You are also worth the time and effort of getting to know the man. If a man can't wait, he is not worth the risk. This is a huge decision and requires time. Who you let in your life can put you and your children at risk, especially the children. It is amazing how little thought people give this, you cannot trust a stranger with your entire life.

You may be a working mother in any of these scenarios. I know that the stress from the job, bills, relationships, and life, in general, can be overwhelming. One of the best things to do is simplify. Less actually is more, meaning fewer commitments and more free time. Eliminate anything that is extra in your life because the necessary things keep you busy enough. You need to decide on core tasks to focus your time and attention. The core things are essential in your life. God and your children should top the list of important things in your life. Children will be a blessing all of their life when you do the work to raise them correctly. They will also be blessed and have a more balanced life as adults when nurtured as children. Remember it is not just about feeding, clothing and sending them to school. A parent's job is about teaching them morals and godly principles. Again, it is about prioritizing and making room for God. Make room for the important things in your life and manage your time. Make cutbacks and do without things so that you have time to teach your children. It is not optional that they feel loved and grow up healthy and happy. Get help, ask your husband, the child's father, your parents, siblings, and friends. Do whatever is necessary to simplify and prioritize your life. You may want to ask a minister to assist you and your family. You may get to know some church families that will help and support on occasion. Find time to read your Bible and study the word of God. The next chapter is for grandparents, but it has many principles for parents to understand as well. It may even give you ideas as to how to make grandparent time with the kids more beneficial.

1 Thessalonians 2:11–2:12

For you know that we dealt with each of you as a father deals with his own children, encouraging, comforting and urging you to live lives worthy of God, who calls you into his kingdom and glory.

The world treats stay at home mothers as if they are less because they do not have a title or a career. Mothers that are fortunate enough to stay home have opportunities to shape their children preparing them for a challenging world. Some mothers have no choice about working outside of the home. Mothers and Fathers should be the most guiding and influential people in their child's life. Don't ever let the world assign your value or importance. Being a mother was the most rewarding and challenging job that I ever held. Hold your heads up, mothers; raising your children with love, ethics and morals is a beautiful gift and career.

The world can be a dangerous place for children. Children need our guidance and protection. It is our job to teach them and keep them safe in an unsafe world. Children are often victims of a corrupt society. A final caution to both parents is to be aware of the people who have access to your children. Pay attention to anyone who pays too much attention to your children. The world can be full of predators, and they often hide in plain sight. There is a process of grooming children that allows adults to get close to children. This can happen online or can be a relative or a close friend. It will always be someone who has access to your child or is attempting to get access to an innocent child. It is a parent's responsibility to be aware of the warning signs and not to ignore them. Protecting young children from predators is a must and cannot be taken lightly. Children are victims of abuse because they are small and offer little resistance. It is our job to protect them and to help them grow into well-adjusted adults. Always be aware of people in your child's life. As your children get older, pay attention to their friends and social circle. Good children can be misled by ungodly people. We must remain vigilant guiding and protecting our children.

Chapter 9

A Grandparent's Purpose

We as grandparents still have a purpose and need to help other generations. We may have worked hard all of our lives, but we are not finished. Many of us may have worked hard outside the home or in the home raising a family. We may have saved for retirement and feel like we deserve to rest. The truth is that our children and grandchildren are in distress because we failed to put God first and teach them godly principles. We were distracted by things and money and made many compromises. The world needs us to be unselfish and take the time to show our grandchildren values. The world is overstressed, and we need to help lighten the load. We are urgently needed as long as we have a breath of life. We need to be unselfish and forget the American dream of retirement. Retirement is an illusion and a worldly concept. As long as we have a life, we should be useful to God.

Worldly Grandparents

As worldly grandparents, we love and spoil our grandchildren and then we send them home. We buy them things and spend time with them. We believe this is all we need to do in their lives. We take them to a movie and buy them popcorn and a drink. After the movie, we may buy them a stuffed animal or take them to get a hamburger. We enjoyed our grandchildren, and they had a good time. We may have been a little stressed, but they had a good day. They will have fond memories of the time with Grandma and/or Grandpa. Many of us help with babysitting and other things for our children and grandchildren.

In a perfect world, it probably would have been enough. It is not enough in the world that children are growing up in today. Believe it or not, it does not help them with their lives at all. It may help grandparents feel loved and create some good memories for the children after we are gone. It does not teach or guide them through their lives. I know you are probably wonderful grandparents by the world's standards. You may even argue that you have done so much more than your parents or grandparents. The world has changed since the innocent days of our parents and grandparents. Today, kids are bombarded with media and worldly thoughts and suggestions. Often, both parents are working, and children are put last due to the stresses of life. The pressure of growing up in this world is incomprehensible, the innocent time of being a child is gone. There is little time for children to play or be a child. The world is speeding at them at an unmanageable speed.

Parents are often fighting over money or other pressures in life. Children have front-row seats to arguments and violence at home. Parents are frustrated and genuinely do not know how to manage their lives. It is no wonder that parents don't know how to handle all the stress, because they have not been taught. Parents have not been taught godly values or how to manage in a corrupt world. The pain and suffering keep accumulating from generation to generation. In addition to the stress and pain at home, children are exposed to even more through the media. Children are often exposed to violence through the television, internet, and video games. While their minds are developing, their innocence is being taken away and replaced with images through media.

Children are in survival mode which causes them to be selfish. Children are bombarded with television commercials and ads. These ads are designed to make the children want worldly products desperately. It creates a desire for worldly possessions and greed. Parents and grandparents often buy children everything they want to make them "happy." Earthly possessions temporarily provide a sense of happiness. In the end, it is an illusion, once the child tires of the toy they need something else to create a sense of happiness. Parents and grandparents believe that they show love to children when they buy them things, but the children are never satisfied. The reason that they are never satisfied is that their real need is not toys.

It is strange that children become selfish for toys and possessions but have no real identity. Children do not know who they are in this world. Children identify with possessions as their identity. One child may feel superior because they have nice clothes or their parents have a lovely home. When children go to school and get good grades, we tell them that they are so smart. When children look cute in an outfit, we tell them that they are beautiful or handsome. We are reflecting what they are on the outside. We are meeting the needs of their minds and bodies with food and clothing. We are failing to connect with children on a deeper spiritual level. We are failing to teach them how to love one another, have patience, and endure healthy suffering. Suffering is crucial because it helps to develop character. When I say suffering, I am not saying to ever harm a child. I am not saying to withhold love or food or to cause them any pain. If they do not get the new toy, it will not harm them, and it may build their character and teach them the value of money. The point is, what life lessons are you teaching your grandchildren? When they get everything they want as children, they grow up expecting that everything will magically appear. They are devastated to find out that they have to work to get things when they grow up. Wouldn't it be kinder to let them do chores around your home and teach them good work values? Wouldn't it be wonderful if they felt a sense of pride in a job well done? It would help to teach them good work ethics and character.

As grandparents, we are wiser and have learned many life lessons. We have the time to read our Bible and extract even more wisdom to guide our children and grandchildren. We can be a source of knowledge and help to a lost world. We need to ask ourselves if we are living for ourselves, or if God still has a plan for us. Retirement is a man-made idea; there is no mention of it in the Bible. There is always something we can do for God. The shape our society is in makes it clear; we need all the help that we can find. I am sorry, but we have been called back to active duty. Find a purpose for your life and do the work for God. Help a damaged struggling world and provide whatever healing and guidance that you can. As we age, we still have a purpose both as a parent and a grandparent. When we look beyond ourselves, we can see an entire world in desperate need of help. There is always someone in need even if you did not have children or if they do not live close. We can use the internet to reach people far away. Good intentions without actions will not help a lost and hurting world. Begin to challenge yourself and ask what contributions you can make. We can send e-mails to television producers or stations requesting responsible entertainment. We can write to government officials asking them to look at the imbalance in our legal system. We can help a single mother with groceries for a week. We need to find a use and purpose for our lives. We must use the gifts that God has given for the betterment of all humankind. Excuses will not help anyone and actions are required.

Boundaries

Boundaries are an essential part of this. The number one rule is that you need to do everything in *love*. We are never to manipulate or force anyone to do our will. It is *always* God's will that we seek.

Our children are grown adults and are most likely married, so you have to consider the parent's feelings and respect their authority. Even when their values or plans are different from our own. We need to first learn godly principles and live those examples. Different religious views can be a touchy subject; this is not about forcing your opinions on the children or their parents. It is not that complicated. This is as simple as teaching the child to share or tell the truth. It is about taking time to build a relationship based on trust and honesty with the child. We may want to teach the child to connect with nature and take a hike in the woods. The point is to stop buying things for the child and spend real meaningful time with them imparting our wisdom or work ethics and godly examples.

We must never disrespect our grandchild's parents. This is not about power or control. It is about being a blessing to the child and his or her parents. When a parent says no to the child or us, respect their authority. It is about cooperating and adding to the child's development not creating another war zone for the child. Always examine your motives and ask yourself if what you are doing is in the best interest of the child. We can be right in an argument, or we can concede for the benefit of the child and family. Always put love first, and we can navigate this easily. Manipulation and deception are always revealed and cause tremendous damage to relationships. Love one another! We are trying to create love, hope, and peace. Any other motives will do the opposite. There is only one agenda, and it is to love, guide and support a child and their parents. Our agenda needs to be one of love and self-sacrifice. When our intentions are pure, it will be received by the child and their parents as love and not control. We do not get to determine the child's religious beliefs, that is for the parents to decide. We can have our own religious beliefs and through love and honesty be a living example of our belief system. It takes work to support and bless our families. We may want to host Sunday dinners and ask everyone to bring a dish. We may want to offer to babysit for a weekend and enjoy quality time with our grandchildren while their parents get some much-needed rest. This world is stressful for all of us, and we need to help carry each other's burdens. When we do things out of love and support, it makes the world a better place. We must be aware that everyone is overburdened and suffering. When we get beyond our agenda and our own pain, we will see opportunities to help others.

Galatians 6:2

Carry each other's burdens, and in this way, you will fulfill the law of Christ.

We will need to trust the Holy Spirit to guide us toward balance when offering to help with other people's burdens. If it feels like we are getting taken advantage of because of our goodness and willingness to help, we need to set boundaries. The people we are helping may not have godly values and operate with their own worldly values. They may see our goodness as weakness and take advantage. If this happens, we may get discouraged and want to give up. This is when we need to set the boundaries according to what we are willing and able to do. Do not allow someone with worldly values to take advantage of your goodness or faith. It is a fine line; we must love people in spite of their worldly values, but we are strong and know the difference. Do not argue with someone who is taking advantage of your help. You can just state the days that you are willing to help and set clear boundaries. Continue to help on those days and remember that the focus is on creating a loving, stable environment for children. Dealing with family members can be difficult if they have worldly values. Do what you feel led to do, and that is all. Do not get caught in personal opinions and worldly disputes. Politely tell your family what you are willing and able to do and set the boundaries. Unfortunately, there are still people who will not appreciate your goodness and try to push to get more. This is why it is so important to teach children to be thankful for what they receive and not to expect more. We live in a complicated world, but we still need to be an example. We cannot give up because it may be difficult. Children need us to deal with the difficult situations to mature and set godly examples for them and their parents.

We have to remember that this is where the problems began for us. Too many people compromised or took the easy way out. We were misled by desiring money and possessions. We did not sow morals or ethics into our children. Society has all but eliminated ethics and morals, and we are paying the price. Our children are paying the ultimate price for our failures. It seems that every generation gets worse and has a more difficult life. We grandparents know that life was not always this way. Life was much simpler when we were children. Looking back, we can see the changes from our childhood, to our children, and now our grandchildren. The changes have been fast and numerous because of advances in technology.

I still take my grandchildren to movies, but I talk to them during the drive. On the way to the movie, we talk about what is happening in their lives. On the way home, we talk about their favorite part of the movie and what they learned. There may have been a scene where someone did something nice, and we talk about how it made the other person feel. We talk about it when someone does something wrong and what they should have done instead. We are always teaching and setting an example to children. I try to invest love and lessons in all the lives of my grandchildren. I realize that they are going to face many challenges and I am trying to help them. We know what challenges children will meet in the world. Somehow, we have disconnected and don't feel that we have anything to offer. We may think that we have less to offer because children are better at electronic devices. The truth is that we have much to offer in preparing them for life. We can teach them honesty and godly values. We should ask ourselves "What can I teach my grandchild that will help them in this world?" We really need to change our mindset from outdated to becoming a powerful resource. Even if it appears that a child is not receptive, we can continue to plant seeds. We must continue in faith even when we cannot see immediate results. Faith is believing in what we cannot see. Our personal walk and journey are our choice. We will always find a purpose and a need to fill when we look with our whole heart.

One of my grandsons was bullied at school. His parents did an excellent job of dealing with the school and supporting him. I tried to explain to him that when other children are not treated well at home, they often come to school angry. I let him know that it had nothing to do with him and that the other boy had suffered a great deal of pain because of his parents. He was able to understand and move on from the situation with a better understanding of another person's pain.

When I talk to my grandchildren, we often talk about saying no to drugs and how drugs can destroy their lives. I have taught them that pain and challenges will come, but that drugs only add to the problems. We have discussed how we need to stand up to the pain instead of hiding from it or numbing the pain. We have talked about being able to work through problems and developing the skills to handle life. We have talked about the way's drugs destroy lives and families. I have talked to them about friends who may offer them drugs or alcohol. I have told them that they are to be leaders and not followers. I have made it clear that they should be their own person, and not follow other people who may be lost and hurting. These conversations are not awkward because my grandchildren know that I genuinely care about their lives.

The opportunities to plant seeds and guide them are endless. It is a labor of love, it is work, but you enjoy the work. Looking at the world from a grandparent's viewpoint, we can see many opportunities to guide and plant seeds to help children overcome the world. Many people have opportunities to make contributions to guide their grandchildren. You may need to read this chapter and others over again to really understand the need to help your grandchildren. You may need to reread it when you feel like giving up. I saw a billboard yesterday; it was two pictures of a forest, side by side. One side had a beautiful, lush green forest. The other side had been stripped by humans. It was a forest destroyed by humans taking the trees and not replanting. The caption over the two photos read "EPIC FAIL." Yes, it is an epic failure, but it pales in comparison to the epic failure that we have created as human beings. It pales in comparison to our epic failure in preparing our children and grandchildren.

The purpose for having children is not to fill a maternal or paternal need to have a baby. Your desire to love a child can get lost in the stress of the world. The real job for a parent and grandparent is to love, protect and prepare children for life. It requires work and sacrifice and needs to be done daily.

You may even wonder where to begin. It is an excellent indication that you have a desire to help and guide your family. Families have many different personalities involved and require love and patience. You may want to start by talking to your child and their spouse about your desire to help. You may want to let them read this book or provide them with a copy. It would help if they could understand why it is so vital to unify to support the children and the family. You may take small steps at first and see little change. You may be discouraged and not see the progress in your family that you had hoped to see. Continue in love, because some of these behaviors are deeply rooted. Love is powerful enough to heal the hardest heart. The value of prayer for your family cannot be underestimated. Pray for your children and grandchildren daily. Patience is necessary, and over time you will see the fruits of your labor. You cannot force anyone to change. You can offer them love and hope and be an example to your family. You do not have the power to change anyone. Change is an internal process and a personal choice. You can guide, support and sometimes cheer a person to make positive decisions. Plant seeds and they will grow. Don't stand and wait to see them grow, just keep planting.

2 Corinthians 13:11

Finally, brothers and sisters, rejoice! Strive for full restoration, encourage one another, be of one mind, live in peace. And the God of love and peace will be with you.

Our families are very complicated because the world has shaped and molded their lives. It is important to remember that the world is in this condition because we failed to keep God first in our lives. We failed to follow the examples of Jesus Christ. You may have had a beautiful son or daughter that was very sweet and amazing as a child. As an adult, you may not be able to recognize them as that sweet innocent child any longer. We may have not realized the importance of sowing godly morals and values then, but we realize it now. The only power and hope that we have for our children and grandchildren are to be a guiding light. The world has hardened their hearts, and they may be overwhelmed with life. What we can do to help them is to read and study our Bibles. This is to get an understanding of godly scriptures and principles. These are the seeds that we can quietly and lovingly sow into their lives. Some people may be so lost in the world that they feel attacked or judged by a Christian. We have to remember that worldly people measure and judge everything. Worldly people may not understand pure love and the willingness to help. Worldly people aren't able to comprehend godly love or hope. People lost in the world can't comprehend what is wrong with the world. The last thing worldly people need is a person telling them how wrong they are living their lives. The Bible instructs us to gently guide and help others. Christians must remember that it is God's will and not our own that we are seeking. We can humbly and quietly seek God and serve him.

When we seek first to become mature, we will be able to gently plant seeds of godly wisdom. The place to begin is with ourselves, seeking to mature and gain a full understanding of godly love and knowledge.

Chapter 10

Pick Up Your Cross

1 Peter 2:24–2:25

"He himself bore our sins" in his body on the cross, so that we might die to sins and live for righteousness; "by his wounds you have been healed." For "you were like sheep going astray," but now you have returned to the Shepherd and Overseer of your souls.

Jesus bore our sins in his body so that by his wounds we have been healed. Can you imagine anything more personal or loving? When we build a personal relationship with Jesus, we must remember what he did for us on the cross. We have all been lost sheep in the world. We have all gone astray and gone along with the world at some point in our lives. We are at a different point now because we now know the truth and the way. We are able to live in righteousness and to turn away from the emptiness of the world. Jesus is our Shepherd, so it makes sense to follow him and remain close so that he can lead and care for us.

John 14:6

Jesus answered, "I am the way and the truth and the life. No one comes to the Father except through me."

It is no longer acceptable to live as the world lives. We have been called to a higher purpose and can no longer live as if we do not understand Jesus Christ. We cannot pretend or deny his existence. It is so simple, if we believe that Jesus died for our sins then we must live lives worthy of his sacrifice. We must die to sin and live for righteousness. To live righteously means to live morally upright without sin or guilt. We have internal knowledge of right from wrong. We merely have to do what is right and stay clear from sin. The world makes this seem much more complicated. For instance, I know it is wrong to steal, so I don't steal. No sin, no guilt, and I live in peace. The real problem is that people tend to wing every moment and just react to what is happening in the world. We truly need to define what we believe before we get into these situations. By knowing the Bible, we learn about the traps and pitfalls that will ensnare us. Knowing our beliefs and the Bible enable us to avoid the pitfalls. It also allows us to recognize them and get out quickly if we fall. We must clearly define our morals and boundaries before we run into trouble. If we know our beliefs and have decided to do what is right beforehand, temptations are reduced or eliminated. Being prepared in advance makes us far less likely to do something sinful. How we show up in the world truly matters. Being firmly committed to our beliefs keeps us from being lost and confused in a very corrupt society. Committing to our beliefs and being prepared for temptation is vital. We must also be aware that our sin hurts not only our lives, but also our family and the world. It appears to be a small thing when we choose to sin, but the effects are far-reaching. Notice that it is a choice to sin and we should not take this choice lightly. When we allow ourselves to live in sin, it creates the world we all share. One sin at a time seems small, but when everyone is sinning, they add up to create pain for everyone. We must hold ourselves to a higher standard so that we stop inflicting pain and suffering onto one another. It is time to understand that living godly and free from sin has a lasting effect on our lives and on society. Living in sin without a moral compass has caused the pain and suffering of the world. Human beings need to realize the importance of living godly and morally. Often religious practices seem difficult to comprehend and hard to follow. People have made this much more complicated with rules and ceremonies. Often, people are overwhelmed and lost in the idea of religion. The only advice that I can give you is to read your Bible and choose to seek God and to follow Jesus according to the scriptures. We can get lost in religion, but a personal relationship with God and believing in Jesus Christ will never fail. We need to mature and to become a follower that is worthy of calling themselves

Christians. We cannot allow ourselves to go back and forth between the world and Christianity. We must make a clear commitment to being a Christian. We can overcome the trials and struggles of being a Christian in a corrupt world. As we overcome these trials, we will become firmly planted and will grow strong roots. We will become the mature body of Christ. Fear will come against us, and we must push on with a commitment to Jesus Christ. Fear and doubt are not from God. We are much stronger than we realize but we have been unclear regarding our commitment. When we understand that work and commitment are required, and that fear is not an option, we can move forward fearlessly. Unconcerned with worldly things we will only be seeking God's will. We are empowered when we put God's will above our own will. When we love God with a pure heart, sacrificing our will is very easy.

Luke 9:23

Then He said to them all: "Whoever wants to be my disciple must deny themselves and take up their cross daily and follow me."

You will notice in the scripture above that we must pick up our cross and follow Jesus. We must also do this daily. It also states that we must deny ourselves. We must turn away from selfish worldly desires and pick up our cross. We must desire a relationship with God more than all the trappings of this world and our own selfish desires. We were never meant to be selfish or to seek things for ourselves. We were designed to love one another and to care for one another. When we deny ourselves, it opens us up to love and caring for each other. Letting go of worldly things is much easier than we realize because they don't actually fulfill our real needs. It is possible to live without all the trappings of the world and to be thankful for being given what we need instead of everything that we desire. We must understand that the worldly way of business is about inventing products and selling them to us for profit. There will always be new inventions and things to be desired. We are intentionally made to feel lesser if we don't own all the latest gadgets. Advertising makes sure that we get the message that we will be more when we own their product. Our society pressures us to not fall behind in technology, or we too will be obsolete. It is enough to be able to use a cell phone and a computer, we do not really need the newest technology. Many people do not know how to use all the features on their phones. When our older model really is obsolete, we can replace it, but we do not have to compete in this ridiculous rat race that we call life. We should be working on becoming better human beings and teaching children values that will help them throughout their lives. Technology will always become outdated and obsolete. Godly values and morals have stood the test of time. Jesus is still someone who you want to follow and has been for over two thousand years. We should invest our time and resources in pursuing things that truly matter and will help humanity. We are wasting our time on this earth on the ridiculous pursuit of wealth and greed. Isn't it time that we stop wasting our time? We should live real, godly lives and turn away from worldliness. Isn't it time to sow lasting values into our children and grandchildren? We have been tempted and deceived long enough. We have a choice as to what we desire and allow into our lives. Just because the manipulation continues does not mean we have to buy into the empty promises of the world. I believe it is time for real Christians and real love. It is time for committed Christians to turn away from the world. It is time for Christians to follow Jesus Christ both in truth and in action. We can no longer give lip service as a Christian and then turn away and act worldly. It is time to commit to being and living godly. It is time to say no to allowing sin when it is convenient. It is time to stand and be Christian, regardless of the cost.

You may be suffering immensely at this point in your life. You may have suffered for many years, and it may feel that there is no point or purpose for your life. I am sure this is how you feel if you have been living a shallow, worldly life. How many things can you do for yourself? How many things can you buy yourself? How many different ways can you entertain yourself? When you live in a worldly way, you limit yourself to yourself. Worldly people are shallow and lack depth and character. What has developed is a worldly self that is selfish, deceptive, and manipulative. Selfish people lack empathy and compassion for others. This then leads to such intense pain and suffering that most people try to escape in some form or another. If you believe that you or possessions are the point of life, you have missed the point. We do not get to have things both ways any longer.

Romans 8:28

And we know that in all things God works for the good of those who love him, who have been called according to his purpose.

We are not our own, and we have a higher calling than our own selfish desires. When we love God, we have a higher purpose than ourselves. When we love others and care for others, we have a higher purpose than ourselves. Our life develops depth and width; it has meaning and a purpose. God wants us to love one another and to strengthen and support one another. If we were encouraging one another in faith, we could unify and become the mature body of Christ. When we are selfish, we remain divided and against one another. Lifting and encouraging one another in faith and in love should be our primary goal and purpose. We have been so unsuccessful in supporting each other and unifying because we have been selfish. When we no longer worry about our own needs and desires, then we will be free to care for others. The truth is that when we love others, we get real love in return. The things and possessions in the world are meaningless compared to serving God. There is nothing in the world that has value compared to the love and peace that comes from following Jesus.

John 3:16

For God so loved the world that he gave his one and only Son, that whoever believes in him shall not perish but have eternal life.

God loved us so much that he gave his one and only Son so that we could have eternal life. It is ridiculous for us to believe that life is about ourselves or possessions. Jesus suffered so much in this world. Why do we think that we will not also suffer many things? Our suffering is equal to the things that God is trying to develop inside of us and the sin that needs to be removed. God is teaching us godliness and removing our worldliness. We need to understand that we are not just living our lives, but preparing for eternal life. The stakes are much higher than what we are experiencing now.

Jesus is indeed our example. There are lessons in everything he did and said in the Bible. He was born into a sinful world and felt the need to be baptized by John the Baptist. Jesus also commands us to pick up our cross. We may wear our cross jewelry but not fully understand the example. Jesus had to carry his own cross to be crucified upon. Jesus was so abused that the Romans had to order Simon a man from Cyrene, to help carry his cross for a while. Before the crucifixion, it says that Jesus was carrying his own cross.

John 19:17-19:18

Carrying his own cross, he went to the place of the Skull (which in Aramaic is called Golgotha). There they crucified him, and with him two others-one on each side and Jesus in the middle.

The example from Jesus carrying his cross was that he accepted that this must come to pass. The other example was that Simon helped him as we should help one another. Our crosses as human beings are to turn away from the worldly desires and to accept suffering to mature as Christians. We need to read and study the Bible so that we fully understand how to follow Jesus. We cannot follow him without reading the words that he spoke to his followers. We cannot follow him without accepting our pain as Jesus did. We cannot follow him until we pick up our cross and walk as he did. Jesus died on the cross for our sins and gave us many examples to follow. Jesus calls himself a teacher because he was teaching us what we needed to know to follow him. We have been given everything we need to know to live a godly life through our knowledge of him. We are to escape the corruption of the world and follow Jesus Christ. The Bible tells us that the corruption of the world was caused by evil desires. The Bible tells us to add goodness to our faith. Then we are to add knowledge, which means godly knowledge. Read the scriptures below very carefully.

2 Peter 1:3–1:8

His divine power has given us everything we need for a godly life through our knowledge of him who called us by his own glory and goodness. Through these he has given us his very great and precious promises, so that through them you may participate in the divine nature, having escaped the corruption in the world caused by evil desires. For this reason, make every effort to add to your faith goodness; and to goodness, knowledge; and to knowledge, self-control; and to self-control, perseverance; and to perseverance, godliness; and to godliness, mutual affection; and to mutual affection, love. For if you possess these qualities in increasing measure, they will keep you from being ineffective and unproductive in your knowledge of our Lord Jesus Christ.

In the scriptures, it also tells us to add self-control, perseverance, godliness, mutual affection, and love. The scriptures tell us to possess these qualities in increasing measure. When we keep striving to have these qualities, they will increase. These qualities keep us from being ineffective Christians. These qualities also prevent us from being unproductive Christians.

The scriptures tell us that we need the knowledge of our Lord Jesus Christ. We cannot mature and become effective Christians without godly knowledge. We cannot survive in the world with only worldly knowledge and rely on our own instincts. We will be tricked and deceived by the world without godly knowledge.

The corruption in the world is caused by evil desires. Evil desires lead us to sin and down a path of destruction. It is difficult not to have evil desires because sin and temptation are everywhere in our society. Our society needs nonviolent and nonsexual entertainment. We are not asking that every show should be based on religion. We are asking for creative entertainment that makes us laugh and relax. People are overwhelmed by the decay and corruption in the world. We really need some mental downtime. Movies that teach us goodness or kindness and instruct us gently. Entertainment that just entertains such as a comedy would be welcomed. We do not want entertainment that encourages young people to make sexual or violent choices that will ruin their lives. We must be in control of ourselves and choose godliness on purpose. Life is not a series of situations that arise that need to be survived. We must be prepared and understand what we are choosing. We have the power of self-control, and we can increase self-control through consistent daily use.

Titus 2:12–2:14

It teaches us to say no to ungodliness and worldly passions, and to live self-controlled, upright and godly lives in this present age, while we wait for the blessed hope — the appearing of the glory of our great God and Savior, Jesus Christ, who gave himself for us to redeem us from all wickedness and to purify for himself a people that are his very own, eager to do what is good.

These scriptures tell us the whole purpose for life. Jesus wants to redeem us from wickedness and to purify us to be people who are his very own. It tells us clearly to say no to ungodliness and worldly passions. We are to live self-controlled and upright lives and to do what is good. The scriptures say that we are to be eager to do what is good. Imagine living in a world of people eager to do what is good. The world creates a place where it is hard to be eager for anything because we are often exhausted. Don't lose heart because it is possible to follow Jesus and to be eager to do good.

Most people are confused about being a Christian. Many believe that to be a Christian, you have to be what other people think Christians are like. Newsflash: most of these people are copying what they think Christians are supposed to be like. In some cases, they are mimicking or pretending because they do not know how to be a Christian. Being a Christian is a personal relationship with God. Accepting Jesus

Christ as your Lord and Savior and being filled with the Holy Spirit. You read your own Bible, you say your own prayers. Do not get lost in what the world perceives as being a Christian. On judgment day, you will be held accountable for your choices.

Matthew 7:13–7:14

Enter through the narrow gate. For wide is the gate and broad is the road that leads to destruction, and many enter through it. But small is the gate and narrow the road that leads to life, and only a few find it.

The scripture above warns us that only a few find the narrow road that leads to life. It also tells us that broad is the road that leads to destruction. Many people are on the path to destruction and do not realize it because they don't understand the sinful nature of humans. People don't understand the path of destruction that humankind is traveling. Humans have created so much pain and damage in the world. The things in our lives that we need to put down and turn away from are our sins. Remember that sin begins with an evil thought or desire. These are easy to recognize because they have to deal with lust or greed. Sometimes we are tricked more subtly and must watch for deceptive situations. Each of us needs to stop the things in our lives that are ungodly. There is no compromise here. Either we follow the world and seek worldly desires, or we put God first and seek his will. We cannot do both at the same time. I use an example of building a house and tearing it down at the same time. There is no way to build a house and tear it down while we are building it. We are always doing one or the other. This is also true of our families and of the world we share. Too many people want to have things both ways, they want to have all the worldly desires and then go to heaven. God knows who his children are and he knows who is seeking to do his will. When Christians go back and forth, they lack sincere faith and commitment to God. Believing in Jesus is critical, and we must remember to follow his examples and instructions. As with any relationship it requires work and time to fully mature and to develop.

Much of the suffering and trials that we go through in life work out the worldly defects in our souls. The trials reveal our true desire and true nature. When we study the word of God, we will begin to see if greed or selfishness is in our soul. We will be able to discern what God's will is even when it is not our own. We will stop wasting our time on worldly things and begin to dig deeper to indeed help others. We will want and need to develop a close and loving relationship with God. We don't want to be in the world without the love and trust we feel with God. As we study the Bible and begin to comprehend what Jesus actually did for us, we grow in love and appreciation towards him. We will be able to follow Jesus when we study his examples.

We need to stop expecting that life will be fair. The reason that life is not fair is that we are born into a world of sin. In a perfect world, we would all be honest, and lies and manipulation would not control our society. Stop expecting life to be fair and begin by bringing honesty and truth into your own life and family. The hope is that if enough people live this way and demand it from a society that we can make a change. There can be no real change until Christians understand why life is not fair and commit to suffering through the changes. It is essential to realize that our worldly choices have already caused so much pain and suffering in the world. We are all going to suffer in the world because it is miserable to live in a greedy, selfish world. It is honorable to suffer for our own poor choices and to suffer to follow Jesus. When we turn our backs toward a corrupt society and turn our hearts toward Jesus, we can change the world. We all need to understand that life is continually changing at an alarming speed. The REAL power is to be able to direct the change for the betterment of all humanity. If we were to teach younger generations morals and to love one another, then we will change their futures. There will always be families that fail to teach morals to their children. It would be a vast improvement for all of us if the majority could understand the importance of these values. We have dismissed these values in the past because it was more profitable for people and business to operate without their constrictions. We can now see that these values were given to us for a reason. Without a godly moral compass, we are lost and destined for destruction. We need godly knowledge to guide us away from the harm and damage that we inflict on one another. Our worldly knowledge cannot fix the problems of the world because it cannot see the problems. Worldly people cannot understand that it is our own selfish desires that have caused us to go so far off course. It has been our choices that have led us all to this point.

When we are selfish, we often inflict pain and suffering onto other people. When we are selfish, we cannot see how badly we hurt someone else that trusted or loved us. Other people failed to see the selfishness within us and were hurt when it was revealed. Many may be stuck in their lives because they have been wounded by another person's choices or actions. We will never be free or able to move forward until we have effectively dealt with that pain. We must drag the pain with us every day when we are unable to forgive. Forgiveness does not mean that we agree with what they did or that we think it was right in any way. We must accept that the problem is between them and God. We forgive them for the pain they caused us, and we do not have to suffer any longer. We are no longer judge and jury. We are free to pursue our hopes and dreams. The pain stops poisoning our life and all the lives that we touch. We are free to teach our children and grandchildren all the things they need to know to grow into healthy adults. We remain selfish and unable to help others when we refuse to let go of the pain. When we let go of me, my, and mine, it opens space for God. Our world is small when we are dealing with our pain, and we do not have room for God. The truth is when we love and trust someone, we are vulnerable. It is difficult to find a person who has goodness within them in a corrupt world. We are seeking love and can be hurt to see the selfishness in a person who is supposed to be loving and trustworthy. The problem is that in worldly love we fall for what we think the other person is rather than what they are in reality. We have blinders on to their faults and feel the intense need to be loved by that person. We overlook the warning signs and continue in the relationship. Everyone puts on a false reality at the beginning of a relationship. We often withhold our bad points because of a fear of rejection. Maybe we did not see the person who hurt us clearly because we did not take time to know them. In this fast-paced world, shortcuts are taken, and signs are dismissed to ensure that we get what we desire. The reality is that when we finally know the person who we desired; we are often left with the thought "What was I thinking?" We usually set ourselves up for more pain and suffering because we do not take the time to make good choices. Often, we are damaged by the pain of our choices and the choices of others.

We do not realize that when we do nothing about our pain, we are choosing. We are choosing to remain in pain and allowing that experience to define our life. When we let go of the experience that wounded us, then we have the opportunity to grow and mature. Let go of the weight that is holding you down. You were free all along but just need to let go. People are so focused on the wrongdoing of another person that they are completely shocked to realize that they have a choice to let go.

Luke 6:37

Do not judge, and you will not be judged. Do not condemn and you will not be condemned. Forgive, and you will be forgiven.

Since we are all born into sin and corruption, it is easy to understand why we are all damaged. We need to be aware that sin has injured each of us. We cannot judge each other when we understand that we are all reacting out of pain and suffering. When they crucified Jesus, he asked God to forgive them because they do not know what they are doing. In the same spirit, we can forgive each other for all the pain and the suffering. We were misled and misguided as a society. Many horrible sins against humanity have been committed because of money and power. The good news is that through love and forgiveness there is hope and healing. It is only through a decision to turn away from the corruption of the world that we will be able to heal. If we waver and turn back, we will be headed down the same dead-end road to destruction. We as Christians must be determined to live godly faith-filled lives. We must be committed to follow Jesus and to love one another. It is time for Christians to prepare themselves and to take a stand. We are no longer able to pretend that our sins have not hurt humanity. Not only has it hurt us as human beings individually but is destroying us collectively. We have been so worried about ourselves individually that it has escaped us that we are destroying humankind. Not only have our choices impacted our individual lives but they are also cumulative. In other words, our selfish choices have hurt us all, and they have been accumulating for a long period of time.

We need to find love and compassion for each other. This was never a journey about me, or you. It was a journey about us. It was about unity and becoming the mature body of Christ. It was a journey to develop love and kindness and compassion for each other. It was a journey to develop into the follower that Jesus seeks. It is a journey to love God with a pure heart. It is time to put the worldly desires down and pick up our cross. We may feel that when we lay down our worldly desires that we lay down our control. This can be scary at first, but it is as it should be. When we walk in faith, we trust God to guide and to provide for us. We put down our selfish desires and walk in faith and love. We are given what we need instead of all the harmful things we desire.

Proverbs 3:5–3:6

Trust in the Lord with all your heart and lean not on your own understanding; in all your ways acknowledge him, and he will make your paths straight.

In a selfish world where we scheme to take care of our own interests, it can be frightening to give up control. The feeling of not having control is powerful. This is when we have to trust God even more. His plans for us are so much bigger than our plans. His plan was for us to develop godly character and to care for each other's needs. His plan was for sincere love and truth. Can you imagine the world if we had followed his plan? Instead, we were derailed with our own selfish desires. The pain and the suffering have reached epic proportions, and no one feels safe or loved.

James 4:4

You adulterous people, don't you know that friendship with the world means enmity against God? Therefore, anyone who chooses to be a friend of the world becomes an enemy of God.

The scripture warns us that friendship with the world means enmity against God. The word *enmity* means a state of being actively opposed or hostile. We have no choice but to live in the world. We as Christians do have a choice as to how we live in the world. Again, we cannot live worldly and still go to heaven. It is impossible to live as the world does and grow and mature in a deep loving relationship with God. We must decide whether we follow the world or we follow Jesus. It is a personal choice and one that we all must make. When we do not actively seek God and follow the examples of Jesus Christ, we are choosing the world by default. God wants us to commit to him and to develop a mature relationship seeking his will. We are to follow our Lord and Savior Jesus Christ and become the mature body of Christ. We all must understand that we need to make this choice definitively and live the rest of our lives in faith. We can no longer be weak in our resolve or commitment. Scriptures tell us to resist the devil, and he will flee. Most people have little resistance and must begin to strengthen their resistance. By being firmly committed and developing deep roots, we can resist the devil and temptation. I can promise you that it will be difficult. I can also guarantee that if you do not turn away from worldly desires that you will also suffer. You will not just suffer in this life but for an eternity.

On the other hand, when you pick up your cross and follow the example of Jesus Christ, there is salvation after the suffering. It is ironic that people think that it is difficult to do the right thing. No one wants to suffer and give up their addictions. Do we really believe that we are suffering less by keeping our addictions? Wouldn't it be more honorable to suffer to create a better world for our children and grandchildren?

Perhaps if we fight the fight, they won't have to fight so hard. They could actually have a chance to enjoy their lives and not be in a constant state of suffering. In a way, we need to crucify the selfishness in ourselves to save our children. Just as Jesus was crucified on the cross for our sins, would it not be love to sacrifice ourselves for the children that will inherit the world? I would never compare anyone of us to Jesus. I am merely stating that we need to follow his example. He paid the ultimate price for our sins. Let's not pass our sins to our children and grandchildren. Let's join Jesus in sacrificing our ego, pride, and selfishness. Let us truly love one another as Jesus instructed. It begins with you and the people you influence in your life. Changing the world may seem impossible.

2 Timothy 2:19

Nevertheless, God's solid foundation stands firm, sealed with this inscription: "The Lord knows those who are his," and "Everyone who confesses the name of the Lord must turn away from wickedness."

We must remember that all things are possible with God. Together, we can stop believing the lies of the world, and we can create real change. It is possible to do the work and make it our reality. We must all be determined to turn away from the wickedness.

Chapter 11

The Truth Shall Set You Free

John 4:23

Yet a time is coming and has now come when the true worshipers will worship the Father in the Spirit and in the truth, for they are the kind of worshipers the Father seeks.

It has come to a point in time where we can no longer allow ourselves to manipulate the truth. We must not allow ourselves to be managed by our worldly thoughts or by other people. Christians must be firmly committed in their spirit. We must be willing to accept the consequences of telling the truth. There are also many benefits to telling the truth. We need to understand the rewards of living with honesty and integrity. When we are honest, we can be our true selves. Living a life of truth means no more manipulation or deception. Living in truth, we are free from corruption and of being worldly. We are no longer concerned with what the world thinks or its critical judgment. We as

Christians hold ourselves to a higher standard of being. When we consider how the world judges and the criteria it uses, we can see how ridiculous it is to concern ourselves with what the world thinks. There are rules and laws that we must all follow. Why are we so concerned with what the world thinks instead of concerning ourselves with what God thinks? The world has deficient standards and often uses fear or manipulation to maintain control. When we feel challenged because of our Christian beliefs, we must remember how boldly worldly people push their views. Own who you are and be firm and stand as a Christian. If we have to endure being surrounded by greed and corruption, then the world can allow our beliefs. I had a friend tell me that she felt judged and looked down on by Christians. I talked to her and explained that I was sincere in my Christian faith and felt no judgment for her in any way. We can be our true authentic selves without making others feel judged. I try to show people love and compassion without judgment. We cannot change the past, but we can commit to being honest from this point forward. Be prepared that the world is not ready to receive honesty. The world is filled with dishonest people who are very comfortable with manipulation. We must keep our integrity and not inflict pain and suffering onto others. We can tell someone the truth without offending them by sticking to the facts and withholding judgment. We can only control ourselves and try to guide others. In the end, we are all responsible for our own choices. It is going to be a challenge to change the world. We may not notice the changes instantly. By being consistent and being committed to our beliefs, we will see change. The real change must be within Christians to stand firmly regardless of the resistance.

Hebrews 6:18–6:19

God did this so that, by two unchangeable things in which it is impossible for God to lie, we who have fled to take hold of the hope set before us may be greatly encouraged. We have this hope as an anchor for the soul, firm and secure.

The scripture tells us that it is impossible for God to lie. It is comforting to know that all of his promises are true and unchanging. We can hold on to the promises and know that they will be honored. Being a Christian, we need to understand that we are not fighting these battles alone. We have a Father in God, a Savior in Jesus Christ and the Holy Spirit for guidance. The two most significant issues we face are getting godly knowledge and supporting one another. We must also overcome the fact that we have offered little resistance to sin in the past. When we overcome our fear and live godly lives, the world will change. It is in our everyday lives where we begin to make godly changes. The good news is that when every Christian makes godly choices, there will be resistance to corruption and real change in the world. The scriptures tell us that we have an anchor for our soul and that we are firm and secure. What would happen in the world if Christians were godly and fearless? We all must have sincere faith and love for one another to make real change. Our faith and love must be genuine to keep us on a righteous path. The last thing we want to do as a Christian is to go off unprepared waging a worldly battle. We must have a clear understanding of godly principles and godly love. There are no short-cuts, and we must do the work required for maturity. Immature Christians need to seek godly knowledge and sincere love for a lasting change.

To be Christians, we need to have integrity and to understand the difference between right and wrong. We must understand the difference between worldly and godly. It has never been about winning or being right. It is not about making someone else wrong or inflicting pain. It is not about clearing our conscience and passing our pain onto others. It is about our personal journey as a Christian growing to full maturity. We begin by seeking godly knowledge. Next, we must get over selfishness and love one another. We must also live and speak the truth. It is possible to know the right words and still be living a lie. We must put off all falsehood and live honestly both in action and in words. There is much more to learn, but these are a few basic principles. Seeking God first and accepting Jesus we will be guided by the Holy Spirit. We cannot go off in the misguided attempt, to tell the truth, and think that it is enough. We must manage our lives as Christians in every respect. We must always examine our motives when making choices. We must live our lives with integrity in such a way that there is never a need to manipulate the truth or to lie. The world needs to see Christians that are truly living Christian lives. Nothing turns people away from God more than someone calling themselves a Christian but living in a worldly way. When we know God's word and conduct ourselves with integrity, it is easy living honestly. Our minds can be very worldly and can cause us to feel the need to manipulate the truth. When we are aware that we are being tempted, we can turn away from temptation. Satan can use our thoughts through temptation, lust or desire. This is why we have to take every thought captive and make it obedient to Christ. For example, we may be tempted by thinking about someone or something that we desire even when we know it is wrong. At that very moment, we must make that thought obedient to Christ by acknowledging that it is wrong. The problem with our thoughts is that we tend to follow them. We get an idea in our head, and then we think about it and imagine it over and over. Eventually, we will act on this thought. This thought then leads us to sin and then to the consequences of our sin. We cannot allow worldly or ungodly thoughts to lead us anywhere. As Christians, we are to learn and know what is from the world and what is godly behavior. We have to be prepared to make these decisions ahead of time and not to act on impulse. We are to make our thoughts obedient to Christ and not allow our minds to run rampant and out of control. We know that sin and temptation are everywhere, and we must be prepared. We must be equipped with godly knowledge and use self-control as our second defense when facing temptation.

2 Corinthians 10:5

We demolish arguments and every pretension that sets itself up against the knowledge of God, and we take captive every thought to make it obedient to Christ.

Learning scriptures and being knowledgeable of the traps and tricks of Satan is our greatest defense. We will be prepared for temptation when we know who we are in Jesus Christ. We will no longer be at the mercy of an unjust world. We will be strong Christians and not easily manipulated. We often fall into sin and temptation unwittingly. We were unprepared and had no defenses to protect ourselves. It is the same for our children and grandchildren going out into the world. We must prepare ourselves and future generations so that we are not easily tricked or deceived. We must also exercise self-control and stop giving into temptation. When we exercise self-control, we strengthen our resolve and gain strength over the temptation. We must never say or believe that anything has control over us. The words that we tell ourselves matter. When we are tempted, we can talk to ourselves in a godly way. Our thoughts need to be of godly encouragement when facing temptation. Choose your thoughts carefully and pay attention to where your thoughts are leading you. Your thoughts can lead you toward sin or away from sin.

Trust is closely related to the truth. We all have people in our lives that need us to be reliable and trustworthy people in their lives. They count on us to give them the love and truth that they need to feel safe and whole. There may be people in our lives that we have failed or those that have failed us. We should be able to count on each other for support and honesty. Too often in this unstable world, the people who are closest to us are the ones who fail or hurt us. Usually, it is for very selfish reasons, and often they do not see the casualties they leave in their path. The people who we trust the most are close enough to hurt us the deepest. These wounds can leave deep scars and cause trust issues for a lifetime. It is imperative to evaluate ourselves and consider whom we are supporting and whom we are failing. Truth and trust go hand in hand because we cannot trust people who deceive or lie. There is no foundation for trusting someone who can easily use deception. It is often in their character or deeply rooted in greed or selfishness. We can see the importance of telling the truth and of having integrity. We must not be deceived into believing that our dishonesty will not damage our lives and the lives of others.

Ephesians 4:22–4:25

You were taught, with regard to your former way of life, to put off your old self, which being corrupted by its deceitful desires; to be made new in the attitude of your minds; and put on the new self, created to be like God in true righteousness and holiness. Therefore, each of you must put off falsehood and speak truthfully to your neighbor, for we are members of one body.

We indeed are members of one body. What we do to one, we do to all. When people deceive and cheat, it spreads like cancer and destroys all of us. We must have character and make truth mandatory in our lives. Truth is not optional because deception hurts all of humanity. We are encouraged to speak truthfully to our neighbor. It should be one of the first things we change in our new way of life. When we speak the truth, we cannot manipulate people or situations. We can interact with people in honesty without an agenda. We are then free of manipulation and deception. We don't always get what we want, but life is more selfless and balanced. I would encourage you to make a commitment to always speak the truth. To grow and mature as a Christian, it is a requirement. We cannot be Christians and speak anything other than the truth. There are no versions of the truth, and we cannot bend the truth. We must not allow our minds to justify or manipulate the truth. We must put off falsehood to get deception out of our character. We must put off our old selves, which are corrupted. We are to live our lives in our new selves created to be like God in true righteousness and holiness. We have to be clear that our old self no longer exists and that we are a new creation in Jesus Christ. Our old way of life is gone, and we are to grow and mature as Christians. It is through the trials and holding our ground that we develop deep roots.

John 8:31–8:32

To the Jews who had believed in him, Jesus said, "If you hold to my teaching, you are really my disciples. Then you will know the truth, and the truth shall set you free."

John 18:37

"You are a king, then!" said Pilate. Jesus answered, "You say that I am a king. In fact, the reason I was born and came into the world is to testify to the truth. Everyone on the side of the truth listens to me."

Jesus says that everyone on the side of the truth listens to him. We can see the importance of being on the side of the truth. Jesus is again setting an example that Christians need to follow. Jesus always spoke the truth. Even when he was tempted or tested, he always spoke the truth. There was never a time when any manipulation came from Jesus. Christians need to be aware that we cannot call ourselves Christians until and unless we are following the teachings of Jesus Christ. We cannot keep one foot in the world and one-foot following Jesus. It is not possible to do both because they are not in the same direction. We are full of thoughts and emotions and get confused with life coming at us so quickly. Always choose the side of truth when confronted with difficult situations. Even when the world attacks or deceives we must still tell the truth. Even if we lose our battle being honest to a deceptive system, we did not sacrifice our integrity. The world believes that it can manipulate the truth for greed or power. They foolishly believe that there will be no consequences for their lies and manipulation. Even when the world is unjust, we must always stand on the side of truth. It is a worldly trick to try to get us to join them in using manipulation. Remember to decide on your truth and values and not to let the world change or manipulate your beliefs. We only deceive ourselves if we believe that we are following Jesus while we are still following the world. We are to turn away from the world and do what is godly in every situation even when the world uses lies and deception.

Ephesians 4:15

Instead, speaking the truth in love, we will grow to become in every respect the mature body of him who is the head, that is, Christ.

We read in the scripture of Jesus being the head and his believers being the body. It is time that we all begin to strengthen the spiritual body to full maturity. We as Christians have a strength that we have not realized. We have to prepare for the coming of Jesus Christ whom is the head. We need to encourage each other toward growth and maturity. Our purpose should be to mature as a Christian, and with patience and love to teach others. When the world attacks, we will be standing with our full armor prepared for battle. We must never stop learning, teaching or advancing. We can't settle because perseverance is a way of life. As long as there is a breath in us, there is always an opportunity to move forward. We can no longer accept worldly standards and live in ignorance. There is hope for humankind even though we have followed the world. Jesus Christ was born for this very reason as our Lord and Savior. Jesus is our hope.

Hebrews 4:14–4:15

Therefore, since we have a great high priest who has ascended to heaven, Jesus the Son of God, let us hold firmly to the faith we profess. For we do not have a high priest who is unable to empathize with our weakness, but we have one who has been tempted in every way, just as we are—yet he did not sin.

The scriptures tell us to hold firmly to our faith. Christians need to stop compromising their faith and make a commitment to hold on firmly. Jesus was tempted, and he understands the temptation. Jesus is aware of our shortcomings and our weaknesses. Let us not use temptation or weakness as an excuse to keep sinning. We can no longer make allowances for sin in our lives. We cannot allow weakness as a way of life. Christians are strong and able to say no when tempted. When weak thoughts enter our minds, we must immediately dismiss them as sin and not allow them to control our lives. As Christians, we can no longer agree with the world and sit silently accepting worldly standards. Sin has always been present, and we have always had the power to resist sin. Even though we are tempted, we are not defenseless. Individually we can find our own truth and become righteous by saying no to doing wrong and yes to doing what is right. Collectively as Christians, we have real power. We can come together and change the world by not allowing worldly standards.

Matthew 5:37

All you need to say is simply "Yes" or "No"; anything beyond this comes from the evil one.

In the scripture, it tells us that anything beyond yes or no is from the evil one. It is because when we go beyond yes or no, we get into justifying or allowing manipulation. Our minds want worldly desires and often manipulate us into compromising our no and turning it into a yes or vice versa. The scriptures warn us not to allow room for manipulation or negotiations. Anything beyond the truth is not from God but an attempt to steer us into deceit and compromise. When we know that we are trying to justify or manipulate a situation, it should be a clear warning that we know it is wrong. Every choice matters, and Christians must hold themselves to godly standards. Jesus is our savior and was perfect. Jesus gave his life for our sins. We are to follow the examples of Jesus and become the mature body of Christ. We were never intended to be weak or to participate in the corruption of the world. When we understand that we are to be unified as one body, it is clear that we must be truthful and have each other's best interests at heart. Lies and deception separate and destroy us making it impossible to trust one another. When we get over our own selfish desires, we will be able to love one another and work together as one body. Self-sacrifice leads to maturity, love, and unity. When we are divided by greed, we cannot support the body of Christ. We each have our own gifts and should strive to be a mature Christian. We must dare to be different from the world to follow Jesus. We must understand that it is not just self-sacrifice but also attaining the fullness of Christ. There is so much goodness that comes from following Jesus. Life gets so much simpler when we live godly instead of worldly. Living godly is also better than trying to live both godly and worldly at the same time. There is so much peace and joy in being a Christian. It is exhausting living a life going back and forth between the world and trying to follow Jesus. Life is clear and uncomplicated when we choose to follow Jesus. When we know who we are in Jesus Christ, we are no longer going back and forth to the world. We are clear in our decision, and we are no longer double-minded. It is difficult to live in the world when you are uncertain of your beliefs and try to live both ways.

1 Corinthians 12:12

Just as a body, though one, has many parts, but all its many parts form one body, so it is with Christ.

As we mature and grow in love, we will unite as one body for Christ. We have to develop a mature faith and then work together as Christians. We all have some skill or gift that God can use for his purpose. When we finally get over our selfish and worldly desires, we can finally be useful and powerful. We then have a purpose beyond ourselves. The definition of the word *purpose* is the reason for which something is created or exists. When we ask ourselves if our purpose is to seek things for ourselves or to serve God, we see our direction clearly. We have an opportunity to live for God. We can get beyond our ego and work with God seeking his purpose. When we only want to do something that is glamorous or exciting, we are still living for ourselves. It is always our ego that needs to be fed by human adoration or praise. When we humble ourselves to be a part of the body that does not get all the glory, we will be serving God's purpose. There are Christians that are gifted in teaching or song praise that will require them to serve in a more glorified position. We all do not possess these skills and must trust that God has a plan to use our unique talents. We cannot overlook the importance of all the parts being essential and working in unity. Maturity is vital because we need time to develop godly knowledge and learn to work together. Our first goal is to do the work necessary to become mature Christians. We are not of much use to God when we cannot get past ourselves or the world. The real power comes from maturity and becoming a person who God can use for his purpose. We need to decide if we want to continue in our self-absorbed plan or the plan that God designed. When we stop sabotaging God's plan and work with him, we will feel the difference in our lives. Imagine putting our self-agenda aside and allowing ourselves to be in the flow of working with God. Imagine not being concerned about what the world thinks because we care more about what God desires. When we put the desires of God first, our worldly desires fade away as unimportant. It is as if we are changing the filter in which we view God and the world. By taking the time to mature as a Christian, we develop a clear view of what is really important. We can then understand the problems in the world and why they exist. We can understand why loving and supporting one another is essential. We can see how being selfish or deceptive is keeping us from unity.

When we use deceit or manipulation, we destroy the truth. When we distort the truth to manipulate situations, we live in a false reality. We may think that we have gotten away with the deception only to find it coming up in our lives at a later date. When the person who was deceived finds out about the deception, trust is destroyed. We must never underestimate the power of a lie or deception. People are killed over a lie, people go to prison over a lie, families are destroyed over a lie. God cannot lie or deceive us; therefore, we count on his truthfulness daily. We build our faith on God's promises. We should understand the importance of God keeping his word and for us to keep our word to others. The dishonesty in the world is what makes us feel uncertain and apprehensive in our lives. It is hard to feel safe and stable in a deceitful world. The instability in the world grows from the increasing lies, corruption, and deceit from humankind. The world is in this condition because of our own selfish choices and our laziness in pursuing righteousness. We have lost our way and followed a corrupt society. The few that fought to make a difference were ignored in favor of self-preservation and greed. Many of us failed to understand that the world was going in such a negative direction. We were unable to do anything to correct a misguided society. Christians are often alone surrounded by influential ungodly people, and it can be intimidating. They were able to keep us down because we were isolated and afraid of their power.

The power of being a Christian lie with our armor. Our armor literally protects us from the devil's schemes. Scriptures tell us to put a belt of truth around our waist. Our armor is also the breastplate of righteousness, meaning to maintain justice and doing what is right. Our armor also consists of a shield of faith because it can extinguish flaming arrows. Our armor is also the helmet of salvation, which is the forgiveness of our sins. And our sword of the Spirit is the word of God. We need to fully understand that the word of God is our weapon. It is interesting to see that our armor is preparing us to go into battle. Finally, we are to have our feet fitted for readiness. The power of Christians lies with our unity. When we reach maturity in godly knowledge, we will have power working together. Beyond the self-defeating selfishness, there is hope for humanity. Our hope lies in Jesus and following his examples and the command to love one another.

Chapter 12

Overcome the World

John 16:33

I have told you these things, so that in me you may have peace. In this world, you will have trouble. But take heart! I have overcome the world.

In the scripture above Jesus is telling us that he overcame the world. It makes sense that his examples and teachings show us how he overcame the world. Through the teachings and examples of Jesus, we have been given a path to follow. We have hope to overcome the world through Jesus Christ. We now understand how the world was tricked and deceived. It is time for Christians to mature and become the body of Christ. We as Christians must live as foreigners not participating in what the world perceives to be normal. We get to choose whether we follow the world or follow Jesus Christ. We can continue on our current path and create more suffering for all humankind. We can also choose to follow Jesus with real, sincere faith. What we decide will determine our future individually and humanity as a whole.

Often, money is the motive for hurting or taking advantage of people. Throughout this book, I have called it greed. It is crucial that we don't gloss over the word *greed*. We must call it what it is so that no one can say that they did not understand. The word *greed* means to have a longing for unneeded excess that cannot be satisfied. We can see that the world is never satisfied with having enough. The desire for more and excess leads us into temptation. Money motivates all kinds of sin and manipulation. For some reason, we feel that we need more to become more. It is a lie and illusion that more money or possessions make us more. These are external belongings and have nothing to do with who you are inside. These possessions will fade and become old and of little value. Even if we were to obtain the whole world but are corrupt inside, we have nothing.

Mark 8:36

What good is it for someone to gain the whole world, yet forfeit their soul?

We cannot deny the number of people who have been hurt because of greed and the desire to be more important. This sin goes from individuals at the bottom of society to national leaders. The concern is worse when we consider the moral fiber of the people in charge making decisions throughout the world. Money is not just currency, it is power.

If we choose to take the righteous path and turn away from the world, it will take consistent work. When Christians set boundaries and stop allowing worldly standards, we can make real change. The reason that things have gotten out of balance is that there is not enough resistance against evil practices. We must become the resistance and raise standards to create a better environment for everyone. Imagine if every Christian were to be strong and stand together in unity. Our programming on television would no longer be about murder, violence or other images that children should not be seeing. Can you imagine watching comedies and dramas that were enjoyable and could possibly redirect our thinking? Our thoughts are very powerful, and we have been bombarded with viewing the sinful nature of man. It stands to reason that children growing up on these kinds of ideas and images would accept them as normal. Hollywood needs writers who have the talent to write scripts that are entertaining and build humanity. I am talking about shows teaching lessons of telling the truth or doing the right thing. There are movies and television shows that are entertaining without sex and violence. Hollywood producers want to produce the depraved movies, and the writers know that to get a hit, they must please the producers. Perhaps the television stations and the movie backers need to look for better-quality people to produce our entertainment.

Colossians 3:9–3:10

Do not lie to each other, since you have taken off your old self with its practices and have put on the new self, which is being renewed in knowledge in the image of its Creator.

Making a Clear Choice

In this chapter, I want to make one thing clear so that there are no doubts. We must understand that we put off our "old self" and put on our "new self." We often do not draw a clear line, and we can be tempted toward our old habits when we do not fully understand that we are to put off our old self. Our minds usually manipulate us to make allowances that lead us back to our old way of life. We have not clearly defined what it means to put off our old self and its practices. When we read the scripture above, it clearly tells us that putting on our new self-renews us in knowledge and in the image of our Creator. It stands to reason that the more we put off our old selves and their practices and hold true to being our new selves, we will get closer to being godly. It is critical to understand that we must stay away from our sinful ways of life and all the worldly practices. We often want to live good lives and make better choices, but this gets lost in the day-to-day lives we live. We need to make a firm decision to turn away from our old ways of life and all the habits that lead us back. Until we understand the difference between our old selves and the new creations that we become in Christ, we will be confused. We will be unable to know where our boundaries are and will go back and forth. Christians need to be resolved to put off their old self and all the practices that pertain to the old way of life. We must be committed to the new self and pursue practices that follow Jesus. In this day and age, we must make a clear decision not allowing ourselves to go back and forth on our commitment to being Christians.

2 Corinthians 5:17

Therefore, if anyone is in Christ, the new creation has come: The old has gone, the new is here!

Even more important than understanding putting off our old self is taking our commitment to God seriously. We are weak in putting off our old self because we still lack a serious relationship with God. We are allowing ourselves to be insincere in our faith. We need to be firmly planted to grow the roots necessary to follow Jesus. We can no longer have the luxury of thinking that we are in a relationship with God while we are not honoring that commitment. Many Christians believe in Jesus and love Jesus. The real evidence of our commitment is revealed in our godly knowledge and in our prayer lives. If we have not had enough interest in God to seek godly knowledge, then our relationship is still in its infancy. We cannot have a meaningful relationship with God until we are seeking him with our whole heart. We cannot follow the examples that Jesus was setting until we know the scriptures. We cannot seek God's will when we are still selfish seeking our own desires. If we do not put in real work and effort, we will never be the mature body of Christ. We cannot approach a relationship with God with shallow worldly efforts. We must seek a relationship with God with godly love and commitment. We must be determined and resolve to understand God's will through scriptures. Once we know the word of God, we are no longer trying to see the world through other people's interpretations or our own. Many people get confused in the rules and regulations of someone telling them what religion looks like.

When we read our own Bible and study the word of God, two things will happen. First, we get first-hand knowledge required to build a relationship with God. Second, we choose our study program knowing that it is truly the word of God. We can attend church for fellowship, praise, and guidance but we still need our own relationship with God. One reason that Christians aren't maturing is that they are waiting for someone else to feed them. We cannot mature without a serious commitment to understanding the scriptures. When we study the scriptures ourselves, we get the growth and maturity that we need. We need to feed ourselves through scriptures seeking godly knowledge.

In this book, I have used the term *worldly* to describe people who are following the world. I needed to express the difference between someone who follows Jesus Christ and someone who follows other people in the world. Honestly, the world itself is a beautiful, innocent, magnificent creation. It is only the evil desires of humans that have harmed the world.

Hebrews 3:12–3:14

See to it, brothers and sisters, that none of you has a sinful, unbelieving heart that turns away from a living God. But encourage one another daily, as long as it is called "today," so that none of you may be hardened by sin's deceitfulness. We have come to share in Christ, if indeed we hold our original conviction firmly to the very end.

When we first feel the calling to follow Jesus, many of us go to the altar and are saved. Most of us then are baptized in the church. The amazing love and joy that you feel at that moment are overwhelming. Later, as we go back to our lives, we slowly turn back to old ways and forget the overwhelming love we felt when we first believed. It is similar to a teenager in love in the sense that we do not understand the work or commitment required to sustain the relationship. As new Christians, we are unaware of the work necessary to grow and mature to develop godliness. Many Christians are concerned with how God can meet their needs and forget that we are here to love and serve God. We need to build a mature relationship with God and make a real commitment. Shallow service does not allow for growth or maturity to become the body of Christ. When it comes to sin and temptation, we must mature to resist evil desires.

James 4:7–4:8

Submit yourselves, then, to God. Resist the devil, and he will flee from you. Come near to God and he will come near to you. Wash your hands, you sinners, and purify your hearts, you double-minded.

The scriptures tell us to come near to God. When we seek him, he will come near to us. It is literally our choice and decision to seek God. We often wonder why we are confused in life. The answer lies in being double-minded. We have not submitted ourselves wholly to God. We have not made a firm decision to resist the devil and to turn away from the world. Worldly people want to stay on the fence and allow their worldly desires and still claim to be Christians. We know that Jesus did not live with a double mind. We know that he turned away from the evil desires and corruption of the world. If resisting the world means that we have to suffer, then we will endure the suffering. The thing that we need to understand about temptation is that when we are tempted, we have to say yes to be in sin. When we say no, we were able to turn from sin and deny it access to our lives. When we agree to sin, we are allowing it into our lives. Our agreement is a requirement for sin to exist. We truly have the power to say no and not allow sin a foothold in our lives. Daily compromises seem small, but they slowly degrade our will and eventually lead to more sin. We are tempted with more and more and are lost in a damaged world. When we resist sin and temptation, we can have authority over sin. Every time we allow and agree with sin, we are compromising our boundaries and morals. As Christians, we need to stop letting our minds be double-minded.

Being double-minded keeps us from making a clear commitment. It prevents us from growing and maturing as Christians. Being double-minded allows us the convenience of being worldly while calling ourselves Christians. It enables us to keep the door open to being worldly. It prevents us from making the final decision to live godly lives. Being double-minded allows us to remain selfish. We must sacrifice the convenience of being worldly and be prepared to do what is godly in every situation. We will never mature as long as we allow ourselves to go back and forth between being worldly and godly. We must understand that sin needs our permission to be part of our lives! We read in the scripture to resist the devil, and he will flee!

You may have tried to study the Bible in the past. Your motives for studying the Bible may have determined how committed and successful you were in a study program. If you were living in a worldly way but trying to understand the scriptures, it was probably unsuccessful. If you were unsure of what a Christian was supposed to be, you were also unsuccessful. When we are resolved to follow Jesus Christ, we have a clear mission. Being resolved means to be firmly determined to do something. When we choose to read the scriptures to understand the teachings and examples of Jesus, we will have power. We now know what we are searching to find. We now know that we are to follow Jesus Christ. When reading the scriptures, we will not understand everything, but we must continue to seek godly knowledge. Often there will be a scripture that helps us overcome a problem in our life. The important thing is to keep seeking godly knowledge on a consistent path. Reading the Bible regularly will help you build your base of knowledge and increase your faith.

Revelations 17:14

They will wage war against the Lamb, the Lamb will triumph over them because he is the Lord of lords and the King of kings—and with him will be his called, chosen and faithful followers.

The question is, have we been faithful followers? The world does not understand what it means to be faithful in this day and age. As Christians, are we living our lives fully committed to God? We cannot cheat with the world and live ungodly any longer. Everything comes down to a final decision in the end. We get to choose how we live our lives and whom we will follow. As Christians, we have to take being faithful and fully committed seriously. The world manipulates many situations, but on this point, we must be clear. This is not a decision to put off until we get older and make a deathbed decision. We can live our lives being faithful and committed to God. We can have an impact on society and on the world. Choosing to be a Christian and choosing to follow Jesus Christ is an internal decision. Often the external things in life change and bombard us with all kinds of grief. It is crucial that we make an internal decision to follow Jesus regardless of what is happening in the world. We must work internally to grow and mature in our spirit which is inside of us. We cannot let the corruption of the world which is happening on the outside determine who we are on the inside. Regardless of anything going on in our lives, we must become stable and mature in our spirit. We know very well of the corruption and greed that are in the world. When we are mature in our spirit, we choose not to be involved in worldly distractions. Instead, we seek godly knowledge which allows us to understand what is happening in the world.

When we seek knowledge from the scriptures, we become mature and able to handle all the problems and hold steadfast to our faith. Mature Christians are knowledgeable and secure in whom they are in Jesus Christ. Mature Christians are not reactive to the world but instead active in the world. When we are no longer reacting to the corruption of the world, we are free to actively serve God. When we are no longer weak and confused by the manipulation of the world, we can be strong and courageous following Jesus. When we are no longer selfish, we can love and care for each other. Mature Christians are able to gently guide and instruct others to help them understand the challenges of the world. Gently teaching and setting an example as to how to live godly in a corrupt world. Being a Christian means that we no longer live for ourselves. Christians are filled with an overwhelming love for God and Jesus and are filled with the Holy Spirit. Christians care for others and have a heart for helping others without judgment. Christians are unable to lie or to manipulate the truth for any reason. It is okay if we feel separate and apart from the world because we should live as foreigners not participating in worldliness. Christians need to be teaching their children and grandchildren selflessly.

Christians may be thinking that sounds amazing but how do I really find this power? The truth is that we have been given the power through following Jesus Christ and reading the scriptures. We must have godly knowledge and be committed to seeking God with a sincere heart. Many people believe in God and Jesus Christ. Many have failed to be committed to seeking the knowledge of God through scriptures to allow their relationship to grow and mature. Calling ourselves Christians without reading the word of God is premature. We need to understand who God is through the scriptures. We need to understand and follow the examples that Jesus came to teach. We need to love God with a deep, committed godly love. Worldly love is shallow and is self-serving. Godly love is pure and seeks to love and serve others. Being worldly we have not understood how to love God with godly love. It is through maturity and godly knowledge that we can love God. Studying the scriptures seriously, with the right motives is key to obtaining godly knowledge. Godly knowledge is the knowledge of God written in the scriptures. Righteousness merely is doing what is good and right without exception. Somehow the world has managed to make this so complicated.

Titus 1:16

They claim to know God, but by their actions they deny him. They are detestable, disobedient and unfit for doing anything good.

When people claim to know God but deny him by their actions, it is clear that they are living a lie. If we claim to be Christians, our actions must reflect those beliefs. If our beliefs and actions are not following Jesus Christ, we are deceiving ourselves. We can see clearly that it is not possible to love God while still holding onto the world. People of the world are selfish and only concerned with their own desires. It is impossible to concern oneself with the will of God when they cannot see anything beyond their own will and desires. Christians must mature and develop a firm resolve to seek God and his will. Many immature Christians try to be good but fail very soon because they are still only seeking God with minimum effort and sacrifice. Many people want to follow Jesus until it gets difficult or until they desire something worldly. Immature Christians seek God and follow Jesus until their faith runs out. It runs out because they have not done the work necessary to sustain their faith. Immature Christians cannot overcome on their own knowledge and understanding. Mature Christians seek God and follow Jesus prepared and fully aware of the sacrifices and blessings. Fully mature Christians have done the work internally and are not dismayed by the constant turbulence of an unstable world. Mature Christians continually recharge their faith and have the godly knowledge to overcome the world. Mature Christians are empowered and enabled to serve a loving God. Mature Christians have made the commitment to God and are resolved to following Jesus.

We cannot make a commitment to God that is weak and lacks effort. We will only mature in a relationship equal to the effort we put forth. We are only as strong and mature as our resolve. In this stressful world, it is vital that we commit to having godly knowledge and seek a healthy prayer life. We are fooling ourselves if we think that we can survive in the world or have a close relationship with God without seeking him diligently.

As Christians, we must die to our old selves, and our spirits must be born again. We are also to be baptized in water as a pledge of a clear conscience toward God. Jesus set an example of being baptized by John the Baptist. The word *disciple* means to be a student or follower of the ministry of Jesus Christ. Christianity is the religion based on the teachings of Jesus Christ. Since we believe in Jesus Christ as our Lord and Savior, it stands to reason that his teachings and examples must be followed. Again, when we don't have godly knowledge, it is easy to fall back into our old way of life. When we don't have godly knowledge, we are unprepared to make decisions in life. As Christians, we must do the work to continue in our new way of life. We have to understand what Jesus was teaching and have the knowledge provided in the scriptures. It is no wonder that many people are damaged and lost in a world full of sin. Many have misunderstood that we needed to work on our relationship with God and to continually seek his knowledge. The decision to be

Christians was not just about saving ourselves. Many Christians have failed to realize that we are to mature and encourage others to maturity. We were to have godly wisdom and love for one another. We were supposed to be the kind of follower that God is seeking.

When we think of the ministry of Jesus Christ, we think of his simple and pure teachings. When we follow Jesus Christ, we must be careful not to let the world pollute his real teachings. When we quietly learn the truth in the scriptures, we will know the authentic teachings of Jesus Christ. Keeping in mind the corruption of the world, it stands to reason that we need to read and understand the scriptures personally. It is a personal relationship, and we must do the work ourselves. When we mature, we will be able to help and guide other people. God sees our motives and knows our reasons for seeking a relationship with him. Our desire to love and serve God should come from sincere hearts.

When we speak the truth, we expose things done in darkness and do not give evil a place to hide. When we live our lives with honesty and integrity, the world can be a stable place. Imagine a world where all Christians were living according to the scriptures and following Jesus Christ. As Christians, we must move beyond the idea of being a Christian to living as a Christian. When we read the scriptures and understand what Jesus was really teaching, we will be unified in faith. We will then be true disciples of Jesus

Christ following his teachings. We will have sincere love for Jesus and one another. We will be free from the world and all of the corrupt ideas. Truth and freedom are awaiting those who genuinely seek God with a pure heart. Our journey is to get beyond ourselves and beyond worldliness. There we will find God. Jesus came so that we would have the opportunity to follow him.

We have to do the work to purify our souls. Fear not because Jesus is the way and the truth and the life. Jesus tells us that no one comes to the Father except through him. We can see the importance of following Jesus. The Holy Spirit is our guide and comforter as we go through the process. I will leave you with one more scripture to help guide you on your journey. I pray that this book has helped you to understand and remove anything that was hindering your commitment to following Jesus. I hope you can read the scriptures with renewed faith and determination. It may help to begin with the New Testament seeking the teachings of Jesus Christ. After having a firm understanding move on to the entire Bible seeking biblical knowledge throughout its entirety.

1 John 4:15–4:17

If anyone acknowledges that Jesus is the Son of God, God lives in them and they in God. And so we know and rely on the love God has for us. God is love.

Whoever lives in love lives in God, and God in them. This is how love is made complete among us so that we will have confidence on the day of judgment. In this world, we are like Jesus.

I hope that you understand that God is love. I hope you understand the difference between following the world and following Jesus. Immature Christians have shallow prayer lives in thinking about their own needs. When we mature, we think about God's will and desire. When we grow in full maturity and are filled with the Holy Spirit, we will overcome the world. It will be the end of me, my, and mine. We will be able to be the mature body of Christ. We will be a people who are ready and able to serve a loving God. Living our lives with a selfless, godly love changes everything.

CPSIA information can be obtained
at www.ICGtesting.com
Printed in the USA
FFHW021944110919
54937543-60637FF